Introduction to Criminology

This publication forms part of the Open University module DD105 *Introduction to criminology*. Details of this and other Open University modules can be obtained from Student Recruitment, The Open University, PO Box 197, Milton Keynes MK7 6BJ, United Kingdom (tel. +44 (0)300 303 5303; email general-enquiries@open.ac.uk).

Alternatively, you may visit the Open University website at www.open.ac.uk where you can learn more about the wide range of modules and packs offered at all levels by The Open University.

The Open University, Walton Hall, Milton Keynes MK7 6AA

First published 2019.

Edited and designed by The Open University.

Typeset by The Open University.

Printed in the United Kingdom by Bell & Bain Ltd, Glasgow.

ISBN 978 1 4730 2395 6

1.1

The Open University

Introduction to Criminology

Edited by Deborah H Drake, Adam Nightingale and David Scott

Contents

Introduction: What is criminology?

by Deborah H. Drake and David Scott

Introduction: What is criminology?

What is criminology? What do criminologists study? How is it different from the study of the law, forensic psychology, or the sociology of crime?

Criminology is a social science, which means it involves the systematic study of human society and social relationships as they relate to problems of crime and criminal justice. It is also a subject that draws on many other areas of social science to try to make sense of the social world. It is sometimes referred to as a 'rendezvous discipline' – where many disciplines meet to explore crime, power, inequalities and the state. Criminology, therefore, can be influenced by ideas from sociology, legal studies and the law, psychology, history, anthropology, human geography, peace and conflict studies, and almost any other discipline where topics of crime and justice might be considered.

The approach taken to criminology in the upcoming chapters is to foreground the importance of questioning. In particular, it questions things that might be taken for granted in relation to crime, the law, criminal justice, and what dangers most threaten people in society (Taylor, Walton and Young, 1973). The chapters seek to understand crime and justice by considering historical, political and economic factors (Young, 2011). Much of the criminology explored focuses on trying to understand the 'social' elements of crime and criminal justice, rather than to understand the individuals involved.

You will explore such questions as:

- Why does crime happen?
- Are some crimes more likely to happen at particular times or in particular places?
- Who in society is most likely to commit a crime?
- Who is most likely to become a victim of crime?
- Are all perpetrators (and all victims) always treated in ways that will ensure a safer society for all?
- How is crime itself defined?
- How is crime responded to?

- In what ways are crime and punishment related to social and economic inequalities?

- Do the ways in which society responds to crime help to reduce it?

- Are criminal justice approaches the best way to respond to crime?

- Are there other dangers in society as serious as crime which are not covered by criminal law?

Answers to these questions are not straightforward for the simple reason that there is not a 'one-size-fits-all' solution to the problem of crime. However, what criminology and criminologists can do is ask pertinent questions, and make substantiated claims about crime and criminal justice on the basis of evidence in an attempt to contribute to deeper social understanding. For example, in many countries, the rates of imprisonment appear to have no correlation with the recorded crime rate at all: prison-population rates go up, down or remain very much the same, irrespective of rises or falls in the crime rate (Lappi-Seppälä, 2008). Recognising such discrepancies between crime rates and imprisonment rates is just one quick example of what criminologists contribute to understandings of crime, but there is much more to it than this, as following chapters illustrate.

Many people are drawn to the study of crime, violent events, victimisation and the means by which societies respond to such problems. The study of crime often links back to ideas and debates about what makes a good society, including moral considerations and the ways societies set boundaries around human conduct (Cohen, 1973). Focusing on crime and its consequences inevitably leads to considerations about what is 'right and wrong' or 'good and evil'.

Although people often think of 'the criminal' as someone else, it is very likely that at some point you will have broken the criminal law: perhaps you have broken a speed limit when driving, or you drank alcohol before you were 18 years old, or maybe you were given too much change by a shop assistant and decided to keep it. If someone is convicted of a crime by the courts, then they will receive a punishment of some kind. You may also have experienced some form of punishment (perhaps at the hands of your parents, guardians or teachers, or maybe through formal legal means such as a fine or imprisonment). Perhaps you have also delivered punishment – maybe just informally to your children or in responding to unwanted or careless actions of a friend. Or maybe you work in the criminal justice system, performing a formal role responsible for punishing people on behalf of society.

Whatever your background or circumstances, a useful starting point for beginning to think like a criminologist is to consider how and when a harmful action is defined as a 'crime' by society, or in criminal law, and when it is not. This is perhaps more complicated than it first appears because while some wrong-doing is illegal, other harmful or dangerous acts are not (Hillyard et al., 2004). As you work through the following chapters, it will become clearer that what a society defines as 'crime' always needs careful scrutiny and questioning. What criminal law narrowly focuses on does not always cover the most dangerous harms in society, and some actions deemed to be criminal change over time and place. This leads into asking questions about which actions and behaviours come to be made illegal in the first place. Why are some harmful and dangerous behaviours illegal, while others are not? Why are some 'nuisance' behaviours illegal and some not? One starting point for answering these questions is to consider which actions and behaviours societies seem to be willing to tolerate and which they do not.

Public opinion on how people should behave and act towards one another – both in society generally, and across different social situations – often varies considerably. Think, for example, about the way people might behave on a busy underground train or a commuter train at rush hour. A lot of people tend to congregate around the doors instead of moving down into the train carriage. Some passengers do not seem to mind this, while others can become irritated and may try to confront or cajole those around the door to move further in. Another example might be young people meeting up after school outside a local shop. The young people see the space as a convenient spot to chat with their friends before going home. But the shopkeeper or local residents might see the young people as disruptive or be suspicious of them. Elderly people or other young people might feel intimidated walking through the group, especially if they are being loud or play-fighting, because it may feel unpredictable or even threatening.

The above two examples outline social situations in which nothing is really 'wrong', as such. No illegal, criminal or harmful activities are taking place. However, they both identify social situations in which public opinion differs widely about what 'appropriate conduct' might be. Thinking about the way different people view what is appropriate or inappropriate provides a good starting point for thinking about problems and conflicts in society. In particular, criminologists consider the conflicts that are at the extreme end of social relations: those that pit one person's rights against another's; those that result in some form of injury or harm; or those that a society has made illegal through criminal law. In the chapters that follow, you will consider debates around some of the most topical and controversial issues in society today, including, among others, discussions on graffiti, crimes committed by governments, environmental crimes and gendered violence.

Criminological imagination
The criminological imagination is a way of thinking that moves beyond taken-for-granted and common-sense assumptions about crime and punishment. It helps create a deeper understanding of human lives, meanings and experiences, situating them within historical contexts, power relationships and social and economic inequalities.

It is important to consider the idea that public opinion is often divided on what is appropriate conduct, even when considering illegal acts. For example, some people might think that personal marijuana use should be legal. Opinions of those who make the laws tend to be divided on such issues as abortion, euthanasia, and homosexuality – in some places these actions are legal, while in others some or all of them are not. The focus on 'crime', how societies respond to it and whether definitions of 'crime' really serve the interests of everybody in society equally, are all part of the study of criminology. The chapters in these books focus particularly on questions concerning who defines 'crime' and whose interests are best served by existing definitions of it (Coleman et al., 2009). Undoubtedly, criminal law is becoming increasingly significant in how individuals and societies define and respond to problems, harms, conflicts and troubles. Yet how crimes are defined and understood is often taken as fixed and eternal. Part of the study of criminology is to question these assumptions (Barton et al., 2006). In so doing, you will start to use and develop your **'criminological imagination'**.

References

Barton, A., Corteen, K., Scott, D. and Whyte, D. (2006) 'Developing a criminological imagination', in Barton, A., Corteen, K., Scott, D. and Whyte, D. (eds) *Expanding the Criminological Imagination*, London, Routledge.

Cohen, S. (1973) *Folk Devils and Moral Panics*, London, Routledge.

Coleman, R., Sim, J., Tombs, S. and Whyte, D. (2009) 'Introduction: State, power, crime', in Coleman, R., Sim, J., Tombs, S. and Whyte, D. (eds) *State, Power, Crime*, London, Sage.

Hillyard, P., Pantazis, C., Tombs, S. and Gordon, D. (2004) 'Introduction', in Hillyard, P., Pantazis, C., Tombs, S. and Gordon, D. (eds) *Beyond Criminology*, London, Pluto Press.

Lappi-Seppälä, T. (2008) 'Trust, welfare and political culture: Explaining difference in national penal policies', *Crime and Justice: A Review of Research*, vol. 37, no. 1, pp. 313–87.

Taylor, I., Walton, P. and Young, J. (1973) *The New Criminology*, London, Routledge and Kegan Paul.

Young, J. (2011) *The Criminological Imagination*, Cambridge, Polity Press.

Block 1:
Crime in context

Chapter 1

Graffiti: art, crime or political resistance?

by Deborah H. Drake and David Scott

Contents

Introduction

Graffiti provides a useful example as an introductory topic for criminology because – apart from when it includes hate speech, is directed at an individual or is defacing private property – it is often considered to be a 'victimless' crime. In this chapter, you will consider the issue of graffiti and the differing ways of seeing it as art, crime or resistance. Moreover, you will be introduced to some of the different ways criminologists have thought about graffiti. Some accept graffiti as a 'problem' because it is defined as illegal and they see it as a symptom of other social ills; others argue that it is a legitimate cultural, social and political activity.

Like many things you will encounter in the study of criminology, it is not always clear how to define what graffiti is (Coffield, 1991). However, for the purposes of this chapter, it can be considered to be a mark, either in the form of a picture, letters or words (scratched, written, drawn or painted). This is deliberately inscribed on a piece of property, often in a public space, normally without the permission of the owner or people responsible for the property. It is recognised that acts of graffiti have existed for thousands of years and appear to exist in virtually all modern cultures and countries. But the nature, scale or seriousness of graffiti is open to interpretation. Further, there is no universally recognised way of recording or measuring graffiti and it is by no means certain that everybody considers graffiti harmful, or a form of inappropriate conduct. For example, the stencilled work 'Girl with a balloon' by the Bristol street artist Banksy, depicts a young girl watching her heart-shaped balloon float away. Originally, it appeared illegally on the side of a bridge, but by July 2017 it was voted the UK's best-loved piece of art (Kennedy, 2017). Graffiti, then, is an example of a social activity that attracts widely differing opinions on how it should be understood, responded to or solved.

In this chapter you will:

- consider definitions of graffiti
- examine some of the ways graffiti as art is contested
- question if the assessment of graffiti as 'crime' always reflects public opinion
- examine the issue of graffiti/street art in relation to power and the state in Northern Ireland.

1 Defining graffiti

Graffiti can take many different forms. It can include stencil art, freestyle artistic expression, and tag graffiti (a graffiti writer's personalised signature). It may be commissioned and legally painted, and this form can include murals, or it may be sprayed illegally on public or private spaces (Vanderveen and van Eijk, 2016). Some forms of graffiti are viewed as 'street art', which can be illegal or legal. Some commentators have specifically claimed that street art should be seen as 'a form of subcultural activity that is defined as unsanctioned visual art developed and/or practiced in public spaces' (Alpaslan, 2012, p. 53). By this definition, street art is characterised both by its illegal nature and artistic form (Hundertmark, 2003). It is thus differentiated from graffiti that is less easily defined as 'artistic', such as some forms of territorial graffiti (which is when different groups claim different urban spaces with tags or logos), vandalism or commissioned corporate street painting.

'The Undercroft', a skateboarding area of London's South Bank, where many forms of graffiti can be seen

However, many commentators claim that there is not a clear way to distinguish between graffiti and street art because the question of what is 'art' requires a subjective assessment. Dutch criminologists Gabry Vanderveen and Gwen van Eijk argue that different forms and expressions of graffiti and whether they are seen as 'art' or 'crime' constantly crosses legal definitions. For example, Banksy's graffiti is often illegal, but his work is often also showcased in art exhibitions or auctioned for large sums of money. He is also someone who is awarded the status of 'celebrity artist' rather than 'criminal'. Vanderveen and van Eijk, suggest that it 'remains an open question'

(2016, p. 108) as to when and why certain forms of graffiti are viewed as criminal.

The public and legal authorities have therefore defined graffiti in very different ways (Duncan, 2015). Graffiti has been referred to as:

- a 'criminal offence' – a form of 'criminal damage', 'vandalism' and a social harm

- a form of 'art' – that is valued for its aesthetic qualities and as a form of social good, worthy of admiration in art galleries

- a symbol of 'political resistance' – a way of sending a message to the powerful from those who would otherwise not be heard.

1.1   Contesting the view of graffiti as art

Graffiti is often seen as subversive, especially by those who consider graffiti as damaging or harmful to property. The physical 'damage' of an act of graffiti may be easily removed – spray-painted stencils on walls can be easily painted over – but it is not just about the financial costs associated with removing graffiti. The content of the graffiti may be political and very expressive, making a clear statement that people may find either inspiring or offensive, but this is not necessarily the only reason why graffiti can be understood as a form of political resistance. To graffiti a surface presents a symbolic challenge to the ownership of property. So, irrespective of the artistic merits, the act of graffiti is perceived as a problem – a threat to the very existence of private property (Cohen, 1973a). One reason it is considered such a potential threat is because it is highly visible and public.

Social construction
A term used to refer to the ways in which people create meanings and understandings of their lived reality through daily interactions with other people and social groups in a given culture or society.

Police departments, local authorities, some members of the public and even some criminologists make no distinction between whether graffiti could be seen as art or as a criminal activity. From this viewpoint, it does not matter how beautiful, well-placed or positive the message of the graffiti is – if it was painted without permission on public or private property, it is illegal and therefore may be prosecuted as a form of criminal damage. So, the marking of walls and other objects can be understood as a form of 'vandalism', and therefore considered equivalent to other forms of disorder, such as smashing bus stop windows, the desecration of war memorials, or the sabotage of railway signals. 'Locking graffiti into the context of vandalism' (Ferrell, 1996, p. 138) is central to the **social construction** of graffiti as a 'crime'.

Graffiti (tagging) that might be viewed as vandalism in a Glasgow underpass

The meaning of 'vandalism'

Vandalism is a term used to describe acts that lead to the wilful destruction of the beautiful. The 'Vandals' were originally an East European tribe who invaded the Roman Empire and ransacked the city of Rome in around 455 AD. The word 'vandalism' was first used in June 1793, by Joseph Lakanal in the National Convention in Paris, to describe the damage done to cultural objects, which ranged from sculptures through to fruit trees. A year later, Henri Grégoire, the Bishop of Blois, used the word to describe the destruction of art following the political turmoil and unrest of the French Revolution of 1789 (Cohen, 1973a).

However, vandalism also needs to be understood in context and may be motivated for very different reasons (Long and Hopkins-Burke, 2015).

Criminologist Stanley Cohen has written extensively on vandalism and his work has helped shape the sociological and criminological understandings of this term. Cohen (1973a, pp. 34–51) identified six forms of vandalism:

1 Ideological – vandalism is motivated for reasons of ethical or political principle, for example to send a political message of resistance.

2   Acquisitive – the act of vandalism is accidental, perhaps resulting from a burglary.

3   Tactical – it is part of a wider plan and the vandalism is a symbolic message threatening harm in pursuance of some wider objective.

4   Vindictive – the act is a form of revenge against a given individual.

5   Malicious – vandalism is deliberately anti-social and targeted against society or certain groups in society.

6   Play – acts carried out by children to test the strengths of existing rules and boundaries.

Vandalism is behaviour that violates important rules. Under certain conditions, this rule-breaking is defined by significant groups as being against the interests of society or as threatening the values we 'all' cherish (Cohen, 1973b).

When graffiti is less artistically pleasing or appears in areas where the buildings and public spaces are not maintained, some criminologists have argued that it might be seen as both a symptom and a cause of social 'disorder' and create an increase in the fear of crime (Xu et al., 2005). As a symptom, graffiti may be thought to reflect an undercurrent of discontent or to indicate street-gang activity in a particular area.

Graffiti celebrating the violent teenage gang, 'the Tongs', in Carlton, Glasgow

For those that view it as a cause, it may heighten public fears or increase the chances of other crimes or forms of disorder in an area. These ideas are associated with criminologists James Q. Wilson and George L. Kelling's (1982) 'broken windows' theory. This suggests that when urban areas are not maintained, an atmosphere of disorder can be associated with the area. In turn, this leads to more serious crimes being committed because it appears it is not well cared for, policed or otherwise monitored.

Criminalising graffiti: New York City

There have been different levels of tolerance of graffiti in different places at different times. One famous example is the rise and fall of graffiti in New York City (Mitman, 2015). When graffiti first started to appear in urban spaces and on the subway in the late 1960s, it was not seen as a major problem. In fact, it was not even initially defined as a form of criminal damage but rather an act by 'mischievous youths' that infringed Transit Authority Rules. By the early 1970s, however, it was redefined as a major crime. In 1972, the *New York Times* described graffiti as an epidemic, and the Mayor of New York launched his 'graffiti war' by claiming that 'the rash of graffiti madness was related to mental health problems' and that graffiti artists were 'insecure cowards' (Mitman, 2015, p. 97). Graffiti was redefined as a form of vandalism and graffiti artists relabelled 'enemy combatants'. The 'war on graffiti' and the prosecution of graffiti artists did result in a dramatic decline in the amount of graffiti on the New York City Subway, but it also led to an increasing sense of alienation by many of its younger citizens.

At times, public opinion can be extremely strong when graffiti appears in a particular area. Local authorities might respond very quickly to complaints about graffiti and have it removed immediately, even when it is not particularly unpleasant or is, in fact, considered by many to be artistically beautiful. Here it is evident that the issue of power can play a role in how graffiti is viewed and dealt with. Local authorities may be concerned about appeasing property owners, taxpayers or voters and not so concerned about the graffiti artists, who are often (though not always) young people.

Reflective activity: Viewing graffiti

Do you think that differing opinions on graffiti are influenced by the groups people belong to? For example, do you think people belonging to the following groups – property owners, art critics or young people – are more likely to see graffiti as crime or as art? How might viewpoints be influenced by some other factors, such as political beliefs or economic concerns? What else do you think contributes to such differing opinions on graffiti?

Summary

- It is not easy to decide whether graffiti should be viewed as art or crime.

- Some criminologists have argued that graffiti is a sign of other problems of social disorder and that its presence encourages 'crime' in certain areas.

- Graffiti is sometimes negatively labelled as a form of 'vandalism'.

2 Rethinking the idea of graffiti as 'crime'

One way of interpreting graffiti is to consider it as a form of art. Rather than looking at the act and associating it with 'criminal damage', graffiti can be associated with other forms of culture. As we mentioned earlier, some graffiti street artists have gained great fame and the work of a number of graffiti artists, such as David Choe, Blek le Rat (aka Xavier Prou), Retna (aka Marquis Lewis) and Eduardo Kobra, have made the transition into art galleries or art auctions. For example, Banksy's 'Space girl and bird' stencil, which depicts a young girl wearing a diving helmet looking at a yellow bird standing on her hand, was sold at an auction in London in April 2007 for just under US $500,000. A number of other Banksy stencils have also sold for hundreds of thousands of US dollars (Widewalls, 2017).

Graffiti: Art or crime?

There are certain rules applied to determine if graffiti is a form of art (Gomez, 1993). In a recent case in the UK, a graffiti artist named 'Tox' was imprisoned after a judge ruled that his graffiti had no artistic merit. The judge drew on the expert opinion of an art critic, who had the power to define his work as not meeting the criteria of a work of art.

When thinking about whether graffiti is a form of art, it is important to consider:

- the relationship between the motivation of the graffiti artist and the reception by the social audience (such as the general public, art critics, politicians). It is not just about the work, but when, where and how it was made and whether it was conceived as a symbol of hope, a criminal act or a piece of art.

- the difficulty of judging works of art; a 'criminal' graffiti artist is not deemed an authorised person to define their work as art. A judge, however, has much more power and influence when it comes to definitions, though not necessarily the knowledge to assess this without the testimony of an art critic. But is criminal law too blunt an instrument to engage with issues around artistic interpretation?

> - what is 'art'? This question often tends to depend on who the artist is and where art is displayed. If it is by an authorised artist (that is someone with professional status or has been judged by artists to be a peer) and shown in an art gallery, then it is often considered art. Social reactions of the general public may be negative but the opinions of art critics are important in shaping definitions.

Whether an object is viewed as artistically beautiful – or, as in the case of graffiti, whether it is viewed by the public as art or crime – is subjective. Vanderveen and van Eijk's (2016) research in the Netherlands on public opinion of graffiti found, similar to other studies on the subject, that public opinion on the issue of graffiti is not clear-cut. In short, they found that although, generally speaking, Dutch people had a fairly neutral opinion of graffiti, there was huge variation not just between different members of the public, but on an individual level. People sometimes viewed different forms of graffiti in different ways and, therefore, had quite mixed reactions to it. The researchers found that when people viewed graffiti in positive ways, it was due to *aesthetic* judgements (that is, the appreciation of its beauty); when they viewed it in negative ways, it involved *moral* judgements (that is, seeing it as vandalism, defacing private property, a sign of anti-social behaviour). However, these assessments could differ, substantially, on the basis of where the graffiti was located and how that area was viewed: for example, the extent to which an area was seen as 'edgy' (which was viewed to be a positive judgement about an area). The researchers argued that 'graffiti in one neighbourhood is not the same as the same type of graffiti in another neighbourhood' (p. 118). Thus, graffiti was not always seen as 'wrong' or necessarily as a form of crime, but sometimes it could be, depending on a variety of judgements people made.

So, there are certain activities in society that are technically designated as crimes in the legal system but that might, in actuality, not really be viewed as such by all members of the public at all times. With regards to graffiti, people may feel a sense of tension about its criminal designation because it can also produce beautiful images that enhance the quality of life in a particular area, or make the area more appealing to certain groups of people (perhaps through the creation of an artistic space or 'quarter').

Beautiful street art or mindless vandalism? Graffiti-painted wall of a building, Soho, Manhattan, New York City

Vanderveen and van Eijk's (2016) research on graffiti revealed two key points that are important for thinking about the tensions and conflicts associated with different social activities that may or may not be illegal.

1 Context (that is, the circumstances that surround a situation) plays an important role in the way people view different social problems. In the case of graffiti, Vanderveen and van Eijk found that some forms may or may not be viewed as disorder. Even when it was, some people did not view this as a sign of other criminal activity; it very much depended on where it was located.

2 The researchers found that it was unhelpful to assign certain viewpoints to certain groups, such as the local authorities who represent the public, wider groups of the general public, or those who have created graffiti. In the case of graffiti, they found that there was no clear-cut means of categorising who might have a particular opinion on graffiti on the basis of the group to which they belonged.

In keeping with previous work done by UK criminologist Andrew Millie (2008, 2011), Vanderveen and van Eijk (2016) argued that rather than identifying categories of people, it is, actually, more helpful to distinguish different opinions on the basis of value judgements. Millie (2011) has argued that when people consider whether an activity is viewed as a form of disorder or seen as a crime, they often base their assessments on value judgements, as opposed to strictly legal considerations (that is, whether it is already against the law or not). Millie argued that there were four value judgements that people tended to base their assessments on when thinking about disorder.

1 **Moral** judgements – these could be very basic and could include simply seeing something as 'good' or 'bad', 'right' or 'wrong', but, at times, it could also include legal classifications. That is, it could include the viewpoint: 'it is illegal, so it is wrong'.

2 **Prudential** judgements – these were related to quality of life and whether life is enhanced or made more enjoyable by this 'disorder'.

3 **Economic** judgements – these involve judgements that included either economic contributions or costs. So, this included whether a person or an activity was seen to be making economic contributions to society or whether an activity or behaviour led to economic costs for society.

4 **Aesthetic** judgements – these involve whether or not an activity or an object is viewed as beautiful, artistic and 'edgy', or unpleasant, ugly, and 'out of place'. This could include, for example, tolerating a degree of drunkenness if it fitted with the 'aesthetic' of a particular area.

These value judgements are not mutually exclusive: people can hold more than one of them at the same time. As a means of understanding the differences between public opinion, they offer a more detailed and nuanced picture of the lines along which public opinions tend to differ. It cannot be assumed that people's opinions on disorder and crime differ on the basis of the groups to which they belong in society.

Reflective activity: Valuing graffiti

What do you think about graffiti? Can you think of any examples you have seen that you like or dislike? Which value judgements do you think you might use when considering how you feel about an incidence of graffiti?

Summary

- Sometimes the location of the graffiti is more important to whether it is viewed as a crime than the content of the graffiti itself.

- Public opinion on graffiti is mixed and people tend to base their opinions on value judgements.

3   Graffiti and power

So far, you have explored graffiti as a social issue, which is sometimes viewed as a social 'problem'. This has introduced you to criminology and started you thinking like a criminologist. Many people are drawn to the study of crime, punishment and social disorder because they are interested in why things are the way they are, why people do the things they do, and because they wonder if there are ways in which we could live more peacefully together. Defining the lines along which people assess what is appropriate and inappropriate or which activities are defined as 'crimes' in a country's legal system (and which are not) brings into greater focus the key ideas and debates on how to assess and influence human conduct (Cohen, 1973c).

The nature and extent of officially defined criminal activity and how the state and its official agents (such as the police) respond to breaches of criminal law reveal a great deal about society in general and how power is distributed (Scraton, 1987). For an act or event to be taken for granted as a crime in a society, it tends to be defined by existing legal frameworks, such as criminal law or other legislation. However, these decisions (about what is and what is not a 'crime') rely on the assumption that an act or event has caused enough damage or harm to require a society to condemn it. For instance, violent crimes against individuals, such as assault and murder (which we will refer to in this book as 'intentional homicide'), can provoke public outrage and calls for someone to be punished for causing harm to the victim, the victim's family and surrounding community. In these cases, criminal law is used to recognise these acts as 'crimes'. But criminologists also draw attention to harms that are caused by corporations and the state (Coleman et al., 2009) – for example, the harms caused by environmental pollution or harmful substances, such as asbestos, that cause ill-health or premature deaths. Criminologists highlight these and other hidden harms that have been left out of legal definitions of crime. And some criminologists also question whether some activities that are viewed as 'crimes' (including graffiti) are always as harmful or damaging as criminal law may imply. This leads them to question if they should be illegal.

3.1   Graffiti, power and the state

The way graffiti is defined, contested and constructed as crime or as art is influenced, either subtly or directly, by the way power works in society and also by the rules that are made by the government. Power, in the way it is being referred to here, can be defined as: the ability to influence and control people, ideas and events. When power is at its strongest, people may not even necessarily realise it is being used and so do not question how or why certain decisions are made or whose interests they serve. Criminologists are interested in understanding how power is exercised through the criminal justice process and how it is used to decide what is viewed as a crime – in other words, the process of criminalisation (Barton et al., 2006). The state can be thought about as a controlling influence in society that aims to regulate social relations and create rules – including the definition of crime – to which we are all expected to conform.

These decisions (policies, laws, rules) are made (or enforced) in certain institutions: courts, police, prisons, armed forces and sometimes also schools, hospitals and universities (Gramsci, 1971). Criminologists are interested in who runs the state and how their backgrounds reflect social divisions in society (Hall et al., 1978). In so doing, criminologists have often questioned whose interests such policies, rules and laws serve and how this impacts on what is defined as a crime and how they are punished.

Graffiti serves as an example of an action that can be constructed in different ways – as art, social protest, or crime. *How* it is defined is shaped through the exercise of power, especially the power of those people who have the authority to define what is legal or illegal. When viewed as social protest, graffiti can be viewed as a form of political resistance: a means by which certain members of society try to speak out against the power of the state to signal that not everyone in society is in agreement with them. In these cases, the act of graffiti is often a conscious decision to break the law. It may, then, be a way of publicly asserting that the 'artist' exists and that they want a voice because, presumably, they do not feel as though they are being heard. This can therefore be understood as a legitimate form of self-expression (Cohen, 1973a). Undoubtedly, graffiti is a medium of communication and at different times has given a voice to people who would not have been heard otherwise (Halsey and Young, 2002, 2006).

It is also important to recognise that the very presence and public placement of graffiti invites dialogue, whether it is on the wall of a building, inside the carriage of a train, inscribed into the wall of a prison cell, or even in a gallery. Yet, more than this, graffiti can also be considered as a declaration of resistance – something you will consider in further depth in the following section. Illegal graffiti is inherently subversive because it is a mark applied to the surface of a piece of property that the owner did not initiate or ask for. The very presence of graffiti changes the built environment and the meanings attached to that space. Irrespective of the message it displays, it is there without permission, and so presents a challenge to power and to authority.

Summary

- The definition of graffiti is shaped by the exercise of state power.
- Definitions of 'crime' are contested and debated.
- Graffiti can be understood as a form of political resistance.

4   The murals of Northern Ireland

Graffiti can take many different forms and its definition is open to considerable discussion. You have considered a number of different kinds of graffiti in this chapter. Murals are a further example of works that can be considered as either art, crime or political communication and resistance.

A note on 'Northern Ireland'

Northern Ireland is the official and legal name of the region created by the Government of Ireland Act (1920) and, as the legal name, is used in this chapter. This region consists of six of the 32 counties of the island of Ireland and is part of the United Kingdom. It is important to note, however, that even the term 'Northern Ireland' is contested and is not commonly used or accepted by some in the Catholic population there.

In Northern Ireland, murals – paintings in public spaces – are widely employed by different communities. The island of Ireland was partitioned in 1921, following the War of Independence with Britain, creating the Irish Free State in the south (which became the independent Republic of Ireland in 1948) and a British-controlled 'Northern Ireland'.

As a result, Northern Ireland is home to a divided population. Put simply, one proportion of the population consider themselves as British and want Northern Ireland to remain part of the United Kingdom. These 'unionists', and their radical form, 'loyalists', are also predominantly Protestant. Loyalists are those who have the same political aims as unionists but, historically, supported the use of force to defend the union of Great Britain and Northern Ireland.

Another proportion of the population define themselves as Irish and are predominantly Catholic. The Catholic 'nationalists', and their radical form, 'republicans', seek the reunification of Ireland. They do not want to be ruled from Britain and Westminster, but from a political authority based in a reunified Ireland. Politically, republicans are those with the same political aims as nationalists but historically supported the use of force to achieve these aims.

Importantly, these identities are not fixed and continue to change over time. An increasing number of people, for example, do not see themselves as belonging to any of these categories exclusively and see themselves simply as Northern Irish, or as both British and Irish (NISRA, 2011).

4.1   Loyalist and republican mural traditions

From around 1908, loyalist house painters in the north of Ireland began painting murals on the side of houses. This house painting occurred every year in July in celebration of the Battle of the Boyne in 1690 (Rolston, 1992, 2010). Celebrating the Battle of the Boyne is culturally significant for the loyalist community because this was when the Dutch Protestant Prince William of Orange defeated the Catholic King James II for the English throne, securing Protestant dominance politically and socially in Ireland.

Following the partition of Ireland in 1921, a new variant of Protestant dominance emerged in Northern Ireland. It was ruled by a unionist (and almost exclusively Protestant) government that effectively discriminated against the nationalist (almost exclusively Catholic) community in the areas of education, housing, jobs and political representation. These policies of division helped embed segregation between the two communities in social and cultural life. The painting of murals (as well as other rituals such as marches and the flying of flags) became even more culturally important. Indeed, rather than be officially condemned or constructed as 'criminal damage', the painting of such murals was elevated to a 'civic duty' and legitimated by the state (Rolston, 1987, 1992). The murals sent a message to the marginalised Catholic members of society that these streets belonged to the loyalists. The painting of loyalist murals of the sides of buildings was therefore an expression of power by certain sections of the community in Northern Ireland.

By the late 1960s, Catholics – inspired by international non-violent civil rights movements – regularly protested against discrimination, and campaigned and marched for equal rights and treatment. Following a number of lethal attacks by police and the British Army in response to civil rights protests and against the Catholic community, nationalist support for armed resistance groups (such as the then dormant Irish Republican Army (IRA)) grew. Spiralling violence by both republican and loyalist armed groups marked the beginning of the Northern Ireland conflict.

As the conflict unfolded, the streets and walls no longer exclusively 'belonged' to the loyalists. Republicans had also begun to assert themselves by using murals to symbolically assert control over their own areas and estates (Jarman, 1997). In 1981, ten republican prisoners, convicted on charges related to the conflict, died following hunger-strike protests against the denial of their 'special category status' as political prisoners and their criminalisation by the state. During this time, republicans and nationalists took to the streets in increasing numbers to show their support for the prisoners and as a direct act of resistance to the power of the state. This resistance included the drawing of political messages of support on walls of buildings, including the painting of murals (Rolston, 1992, 1994). This period in the 1980s marked the development of a republican mural tradition. While both mural traditions were political in nature, in direct contrast to the loyalist murals, republican murals were acts of political resistance against, and in defiance of, the British state.

A Belfast mural of Bobby Sands, MP, who died while on hunger strike in 1981

By the 1980s, republican murals had become both a key means of expressing resistance and as a form of communication. The early republican murals of the 1980s largely portrayed the 'armed struggle'.

Military murals, however, became less prevalent as the 1990s progressed. Focus shifted towards highlighting the demands, ideology and message of the movement and reflected the wider shift towards securing a political peace settlement rather than a military one (Rolston, 1992, 2013).

The frequency of loyalist murals in the 1980s, by contrast, were in decline (Rolston, 1994). Unlike the republican murals, many of the loyalist murals painted in the 1980s and 1990s were military murals. These included images of loyalist paramilitaries who had been killed in the conflict, reflecting the significance of this challenge to their previous cultural ascendancy (Rolston, 1992, 1994, 2013).

Older style loyalist mural in Belfast

Following a lengthy peace process involving multi-party negotiations, supported by both loyalist and republican prisoners, a political settlement to the conflict was reached in 1998. This was marked by the signing of the Good Friday Peace Agreement. More than 2000 murals were painted in Northern Ireland during the conflict and subsequent peace process, primarily in Belfast and Derry/Londonderry. These murals provide not only a way of measuring the shifting confidence and beliefs of the two conflicting communities, but also historical evidence of how power is both expressed and contested.

The changing nature of murals in Northern Ireland also tells a bigger story about how murals as a form of graffiti can both shape and be shaped by shifting political contexts. Following the peace process, murals in Northern Ireland have been used for new cultural and political purposes by communities and the state. These include drawing attention to social issues and presenting an alternative way of looking at identity or community or of reimagining the state (Rolston, 2013). For example, between 2006 and 2016, hundreds of community murals were created to celebrate positive community stories and promote more peaceful futures as part of a national and internationally funded 'Reimagining Communities' peace-building project (Wallace, 2016). Meanwhile, a number of loyalist murals have been repainted to communicate a new version of loyalist paramilitary history, with fresh-faced, denim-clad young men replacing the balaclavas and military uniforms of the past.

A loyalist mural from 2018

By 2018, the republican and loyalist political murals found in working-class areas of Belfast had become popular tourist attractions, gaining a cultural cachet not unlike that of the work of Banksy.

Reflective activity: Northern Irish murals

In what ways are the murals a way of sending a message from one group of people to another? What do you think the murals mean for both reaffirming and challenging state power? Do you think that the murals are an important historical record of the changing relations of power in Northern Ireland?

Summary

- Graffiti can take a number of different forms, including murals.

- In Northern Ireland, the murals painted on the sides of buildings were used to communicate messages of both support and resistance to state power, and for other political and cultural purposes.

Conclusion

In this chapter, you have critically considered the different ways in which graffiti has been understood, notably as either a work of art, crime or act of political resistance. At times, graffiti is defined as a crime and a form of vandalism. This negative definition of graffiti as wanton destruction of property is sometimes used as a way of indicating other social ills and social breakdown (for example, the 'broken windows' theory). This definition of graffiti is, however, often contested: works that some people may define as graffiti are sometimes judged to be highly valued as a form or art, and you need look no further than the reaction and monetary value associated with the stencils of the street artist Banksy to illustrate this point. From this perspective, rather than being a problem, graffiti is a positive cultural activity with artistic merit, which benefits the local community.

Finally, you have also explored how graffiti can be understood as a form of political resistance, and the murals in Northern Ireland demonstrate how street art can be deployed by members of different communities as a political means of both reinforcing and challenging state power. The study of graffiti provides you with a fascinating case study that can help you develop your criminological imagination and to think critically about definitions of 'crime' and social harms.

References

Alpaslan, Z. (2012) 'Is street art a crime? An attempt at examining street art using criminology', *Advances in Applied Sociology*, vol. 2, no. 1, pp. 53–8.

Barton, A., Corteen, K., Scott, D. and Whyte, D. (2006) *Expanding the Criminological Imagination*, London, Routledge.

Cohen, S. (1973a) 'Property destruction: motives and meanings', in Ward, C. (ed.) (1973) *Vandalism*, London, The Architectural Press.

Cohen, S. (1973b) 'Campaigning against vandalism', in Ward, C. (ed) (1973) *Vandalism*, London, The Architectural Press.

Cohen, S. (1973c) *Folk Devils and Moral Panics*, London, Routledge.

Coleman, R., Sim, J., Tombs, S. and Whyte, D. (2009) *State, Power, Crime*, London, Sage.

Coffield, F. (1991) *Vandalism and Graffiti*, London, Calouste Gulbenkian Trust.

Duncan, A. (2015) 'From the street to the gallery: A critical analysis of the inseparable nature of graffiti and context', in Lovata, T. and Olton, E. (eds) *Understanding Graffiti*, London, Routledge.

Ferrell, J. (1996) *Crimes of Style: Urban graffiti and the Politics of Criminality*, New York, Garland.

Gomez, M. A. (1993) 'The writing on our walls: Finding solutions through distinguishing graffiti art from graffiti vandalism', *University of Michigan Journal of Law Reform*, vol. 26, no. 3, pp. 633–707.

Gramsci, A. (1971) *Selections from the Prison Notebooks*, London, Lawrence and Wishart.

Hall, S., Critcher, C., Clarke, J., Jefferson, T. and Roberts, B. (1978) *Policing the Crisis*, London, Macmillan.

Halsey, M. and Young, A. (2002) 'The meanings of graffiti and municipal administration', *Australian and New Zealand Journal of Criminology*, vol. 35, no. 2, pp. 165–86.

Halsey, M. and Young, A. (2006) 'Our desires are ungovernable: writing graffiti in urban space', *Theoretical Criminology*, vol. 10, no. 3, pp. 275–306.

Hundertmark, C. (2003) *The Art of Rebellion – World of Street Art*, Corte Madera, CA, Ginko Press Inc.

Kennedy, M. (2017) 'Banksy stencil soars past Hay Wain as UK's favourite work of art', *Guardian*, 26 July [Online]. Available at https://www.theguardian.com/artanddesign/2017/jul/26/banksy-balloon-girl-hay-wain-favourite-uk-work-of-art-constable-poll-nation (Accessed 20 March 2018).

Jarman, N. R. (1997) *Material Conflicts: Parades and Visual Displays in Northern Ireland*, London, Berg Publishers.

Long, M. and Hopkins-Burke, R. (2015) *Vandalism and Anti-Social Behaviour*, London, Palgrave.

Millie, A. (2008) 'Anti-social behaviour, behavioural expectations and an urban aesthetic', *British Journal of Criminology*, vol. 48, no. 3, pp. 379–94.

Millie, A. (2011) 'Value judgements and criminalization', *British Journal of Criminology*, vol. 51, no. 2, pp. 278–95.

Mitman, T. (2015) 'Advertised defiance: How New York City graffiti went from "getting up" to "getting over"', in Lovata, T. and Olton, E. (eds) *Understanding Graffiti*, London, Routledge.

NISRA (Northern Ireland Statistics and Research Agency) (2011) *2011 Census* [Online]. Available at https://www.nisra.gov.uk/statistics/census/2011-census (Accessed 6 June 2018).

Rolston, B. (1987) 'Politics, painting and popular culture: the political wall murals of Northern Ireland', *Media, Culture and Society*, vol. 9, no. 1, pp. 5–28.

Rolston, B. (1992) *Drawing Support: Murals in the North of Ireland*, Belfast, Beyond the Pale Publications.

Rolston, B. (1994) *The Story So Far - The Story Continues: Loyalist Murals Republican Murals in the 1990s*, Belfast, Beyond the Pale Publications.

Rolston, B. (2010) '"Trying to reach the future through the past": Murals and memory in Northern Ireland', *Crime, Media, Culture*, vol. 6, no. 3, pp. 285–307.

Rolston, B. (2013) *Drawing Support 4: Murals and Conflict Transformation in Northern Ireland*, Beyond the Pale Publications.

Scraton, P. (1987) *Law, Order and the Authoritarian State*, Milton Keynes, Open University Press.

Vanderveen, G. and van Eijk, G. (2016) 'Criminal but beautiful: A study on graffiti and the role of value judgments and context in perceiving disorder', *European Journal of Criminal Policy and Research*, vol. 22, pp. 107–25.

Wallace, J. (2016) *Evaluation of the Building Peace through the Arts: Re-Imaging Communities Programme: Final Report*, Belfast, Arts Council of Northern Ireland [Online]. Available at www.artscouncil-ni.org/images/uploads/publications-documents/BPttA_Final_Programme_Evaluation.pdf (Accessed 6 June 2018).

Widewalls (2017) '10 most expensive Banksy artworks at auctions' [Online]. Available at https://www.widewalls.ch/10-most-expensive-banksy-artworks-at-auctions/ (Accessed 20 March 2018).

Wilson, J. Q. and Kelling, G. L. (1982) 'Broken windows', *The Atlantic Monthly*, pp. 46–52.

Xu, Y. L., Fiedler, M. L. and Flaming, K. H. (2005) 'Discovering the impact of community policing: the broken windows thesis, collective efficacy, and citizens' judgment', *Journal of Research in Crime and Delinquency*, vol. 42, no. 2, pp. 147–86.

Chapter 2

What is crime?

by Deborah H. Drake, John Muncie and David Scott

Contents

Introduction

Popular media, newspapers and television news programmes often focus on recurring fears of escalating levels of insecurity, violence, knife crime, internet fraud, children out of control, new forms of terrorism, sex offending, domestic violence and a growth in all manner of so-called 'anti-social behaviours'. This is also coupled with growing concerns about police malpractice, corruption, racism, prison overcrowding and deteriorating conditions, lenient sentencing, lack of victim confidence in achieving a desired outcome, court delays and lack of resources. Systems of justice are sometimes accused in the news media of being 'at breaking point' and simply 'not working', suggesting that the public has little faith in criminal justice processes. Indeed, the ideas about how to maintain 'law and order' have been high on the agenda for all major political parties in the UK, particularly since the 1970s. The equation is simple enough. Criminal behaviour is inescapable. The police should be given more powers of surveillance and arrest to stop criminals. The criminal courts should be given the power to hand down tougher punishments. Only then will the public have their faith restored.

But this assumed taken-for-granted relationship between crime, criminal law and criminal justice is not straightforward. This chapter suggests a number of ways in which definitions, claims and evidence about the nature and meaning of crime and processes of criminal justice can be subjected to criminological inquiry. In particular, two fundamental sets of questions are explored:

- What is a criminal offence? Which forms of behaviour are (or can be) considered criminal and which not? How does it come to be decided that a particular act of wrong-doing calls for a legal response and which acts can be otherwise dealt with or ignored? And how does the general public learn of the extent and seriousness of the 'crime problem'?

- What is crime control? Why are rules or laws there? Who created them? In whose interests? Are the agencies of criminal justice best placed to resolve social problems, disputes, harms and injuries, especially harms caused by states and corporations?

To ask such questions demands, to a certain extent, that you step back and look at 'crime' from a more detached perspective. The issues that criminologists study can evoke highly charged and emotional responses. One way of coming to understand why an action is regarded as criminal is by examining the processes by which laws are made and enforced. It requires that you critically consider how 'crime', 'criminal justice' and other concepts used in criminology are defined.

In this chapter you will:

- investigate the definition and social construction of 'crime' and 'criminal justice'

- engage with the definition of 'crime' and how this interacts with criminal law

- consider the way in which the definition of 'crime' is linked to power relations and social class.

1 Defining crime

The most common and frequently applied definition of crime is that which links it to criminal law. In other words, an act is only a crime when it violates the prevailing legal code of the jurisdiction in which it occurs. Writing in the United States in the 1930s, philosophers Jerome Michael and Mortimer J. Adler argued that the most precise and least ambiguous definition of crime is: 'behaviour which is prohibited by the criminal code' (Michael and Adler, 1933, p. 5). Similarly, criminologist Katherine S. Williams re-emphasised the legal foundation of crime by arguing that:

> [I]t is essential that one never forgets that no matter how immoral, reprehensible, damaging or dangerous an act is, it is not a crime unless it is made such by the authorities of the State – the legislature and, at least through interpretation, the judges.
>
> (Williams, 1994, p. 11)

Again, this appears uncontroversial, but two important consequences flow from such formulations.

1   There would be no crime without criminal law (Sutherland, 1940, 1945). No behaviour can be considered criminal unless a formal rule exists to prohibit it. Thus Michael and Adler can logically contend that: 'if crime is merely an instance of conduct which is proscribed by the criminal code, it follows that criminal law is the formal cause of crime' (Michael and Adler, 1933, p. 5).

2   No behaviour or individual can be considered criminal until formally decided upon by the criminal justice system. Although a dangerous act may have happened and a complaint may have been lodged with the police, an action does not become legally designated or defined as a crime until it is processed through the criminal justice system.

In a similar vein, it has been widely maintained that a number of conditions must be met before an act can be legally defined as a crime.

- The act must be legally prohibited at the time it is committed.

- The perpetrator must have criminal intent (often referred to by those in the legal profession by the Latin phrase *mens rea*).

- The perpetrator must have acted voluntarily (often referred to by the Latin phrase *actus rea*).

- There must be some legally prescribed punishment for committal of the act.

Criminal law and court procedures claim to respond to crime, yet crime is defined, and therefore created, by criminal law itself.

Reflective activity: What is crime?

Why do you think it might be important to consider criminal law when trying to define what crime is? This might seem to have an obvious answer: if a law prohibits some activity, this makes the activity illegal and therefore a crime. This is true. However, you might want to think a little further about who makes the law? Who has the power to define it, create it and enforce it? Can we always be sure that everyone is viewed as equal in the eyes of the law?

1.1   Changing times, changing laws

Troublesome behaviours and some forms of 'inappropriate conduct', such as public drunkenness or causing a disturbance seem to have been treated as 'crimes' by police (whether or not they are recognised in law) for a long time. This means that the concept is routinely applied in condemnations of the 'unwanted' and the 'undesirable'. Think, for example, of some forms of so-called 'anti-social behaviour'. Strictly speaking, in the United Kingdom, anti-social behaviour is not a criminal offence. However, if a person is given an anti-social behaviour order and then breaches it, they can later be convicted through criminal proceedings.

However, criminal laws are never static or permanent features of any society. For example, the consumption of alcohol in the United States was deemed criminal in the days of Prohibition between 1920 and 1933. Now it is considered a legal and respectable social activity in US society. Marijuana possession, long condemned as a scourge in the lives of young people, has been progressively decriminalised in many countries, including Spain, Portugal, Uruguay, Chile and numerous US states since the 1980s. Moreover, certain customary practices in

England and Wales, such as poaching game, only became illegal through the convergence of social class and power interests in the eighteenth century. (The concept of social class is not easily defined, but for now it is perhaps useful to define it as a means of categorising people on the basis of social, economic, cultural, political, educational or occupational status.) From early on, social divisions along the lines of class played a role in defining the law.

An anti-Prohibition parade and demonstration in Newark, New Jersey, October 1932

But class is not the only aspect of power that affects what behaviour is prohibited: gender and other dimensions can also play a role. This reflects that, historically, lawmakers have been overwhelmingly male. Domestic violence, far from being viewed as criminal (or even deviant), was considered quite legitimate through much of Western history. It was not until 1991 that England and Wales was brought into line with France, Sweden, Norway, Denmark, Poland and most US and Australian states by the overturning of a 255-year-old ruling that had given husbands immunity from marital rape. So, as you can see, changes in law are not always previously prohibited behaviours becoming acceptable and thus legalised, as in the example of marijuana use. The process can work the other way too, with behaviour that was previously deemed acceptable being made illegal.

What counts legally as crime varies from one jurisdiction to another, even in similar historical periods. An obvious example is that, while in England and Wales a person can be considered criminally responsible for their actions at ten years old, in France the age of criminal responsibility is 13 years old; in Germany 14 years old; and in Portugal 16 years old. Homosexuality is punishable by death in some countries and openly embraced in many others. Assisted suicide is illegal in some countries and open practice in others. The death penalty is legal in some countries but not in others. In all these examples, crime appears neither fixed, nor the same for all societies and for all times. Rather, it is a historically and socially specific concept (Durkheim, 1895; Hulsman, 1986).

Protesters at the Scottish parliament, demanding that the Assisted Suicide Bill becomes law. Assisted suicide is currently illegal in Scotland, but legal in a number of other countries

An understanding of crime that relies solely on notions of criminal law violation reveals that crime is not that which a society collectively agrees is harmful, but only that which the state defines as prohibited. This opens up questions around who has chosen which activities to prohibit and why. Moreover, definitions of crime that rely only on criminal law also underplay the variable ways in which it is enforced

(Sutherland, 1940). Are theft, graffiti and 'criminal damage' more serious than violations of health and safety codes in the work place? Both may be dealt with by criminal law, but the tendency to view the former as 'real crime' and the latter as 'regulatory offences' may lead people to exclude these latter behaviours from what they tend to think of as crime. Divorcing the criminal process from its social context masks the issue of who makes the law. In turn, this may have important consequences for what kinds of behaviour are regarded as truly criminal.

Summary

- An act is only a crime when it violates the legal code of a country or legal jurisdiction.

- The acts that a society defines as a crime change over time.

- Different legal jurisdictions or countries differ in what they deem a criminal act.

- Certain social structures, including class, gender and sexual orientation influence which actions are deemed criminal and which are not.

2   Constructing crime

As you have seen, defining crime with reference to actions that violate criminal law is limited. Society 'creates' crime because it (or at least those in positions of authority) makes the rules, the infraction of which constitutes crime (Christie, 2004). Likewise, what constitutes 'criminal behaviour' can be equally difficult to determine. The core concern, then, is to explore the complex processes by which agencies of social control (such as the police, courts, and prisons) define certain people as criminal. Determining 'what crime is', 'who the criminal is' and 'what criminal justice is' are questions that are open to debate and their answers are always changing.

2.1   How are 'criminals' made?

Criminalisation is not only dependent on how certain acts are labelled and on who has the power to label, but is directly related to social exclusion and social inequality (Scraton and Chadwick, 1991). What this means is that criminal law is 'made' by people with the authority and the means to criminalise the behaviour of others. The argument that law creation and enforcement are selective and partial is underlined by criminologist Stanley Cohen's insistence that: 'damage, victimisation, exploitation, theft and destruction when carried out by the powerful are not only not punished, but are not called "crime"' (Cohen, 1973, p. 624). Nineteenth-century US entrepreneur Daniel Drew poetically stated that the 'law is like a cobweb. It's made for flies and the smaller kind of insects but lets the big bumblebees break through' (Drew, cited in Sutherland, 1940, pp. 8–9). In such analysis, the concept of crime is viewed not as a neutral, 'value free' concept, but rather as a political and state-constructed one: it has no 'objective' reality. For example, until the early 1990s, activities of the African National Congress (ANC) – the black liberation political movement in South Africa – were defined as criminal. Their involvement with helping to challenge the policy of apartheid (the segregation of people on the basis of their race) and the social and political changes that also helped to bring about the end of this policy, meant that the ANC began to be viewed differently in South African society. The ANC have been the party of government since the end of apartheid to 2018, thus demonstrating the role power and social-change movements can play in defining what is and is not 'criminal'.

African National Congress election campaign rally in Cape Town, 1994 – the first year in which South African citizens of all 'races' were allowed to vote

When considering the role politics and social inequality play in shaping what is defined as crime, it is helpful to consider the work of political theorist Karl Marx. In Section 1, the concept of social class was introduced and defined as 'a means of categorising people on the basis of social, economic, cultural, political or educational status'. The concept can also be thought about as relating to property ownership, financial means and social status. For example, Marx differentiated between the ruling classes (essentially, those with money, property and/ or power, including political power) and the working classes (those who must work for a living, or 'sell their labour', probably do not own property and are, relatively, less powerful) (Marx and Engels, 1932).

Sociologist and criminologist William Chambliss (1975) developed a Marxist theory of crime and criminal law, which argued that acts are defined as criminal only when it is in the interests of the ruling class to define them as such. An action only becomes prohibited by criminal law when those who hold power in society decide that it should be illegal. Chambliss argued that it is important to question whether those who make the laws have a vested interest in them. That is, if some behaviours are prohibited in order to maintain political or social control and to counter any perceived threat to ruling-class authority. Chambliss' arguments may appear extreme, and it might be argued that his analysis of the law is too broad and not sufficiently nuanced. However, his arguments underscore the importance of the concept of power. Thinking about who has the power to make the law is part of a deeper understanding of how criminals are 'made'.

Reflective activity: Power and the law

Do you think that power relations in society play a role in lawmaking, or do you view the law as a neutral set of rules intended to protect the whole of society equally? It is not a problem if, on reflection, you find that you subscribe to the latter view. Alternatively, it may be that you find a mid-way view on the law more persuasive, where you can recognise both the interests of the powerful in lawmaking as well as the functions it can serve in terms of public protection. Part of social-science study includes questioning different points of view, considering the available evidence, and then making your own claims and arguments based on this evidence.

2.2   Crime as an ideological concept

One example of laws that can be seen as maintaining social divisions and the power of the ruling class are public order offences. These include such activities as rioting and disorderly conduct. Although it can be argued that these activities can sometimes result in dangerous or damaging outcomes, they can sometimes also to be a sign of civil unrest or protest against the way society is structured. In addition, there are also other public order offences, such as doing graffiti, public drunkenness and begging, that might be seen as more subtly aimed at maintaining existing social and political power structures.

As you saw in Chapter 1, graffiti is a sort of crime that can be thought about in various ways. That is, it may be a crime (graffiti is legally defined as criminal damage), but it is also always something else, such as art, political protest, an expression of free speech and so on (Brighenti, 2010). In a similar way, consider the 'problems' of public drunkenness or begging. On the one hand, you could argue that these are simply individual problems, and that the person who is drunk or is begging must simply find the resources to sort them out themselves. On the other hand, these activities could be viewed as symptoms of social 'illness' (sometimes also referred to in criminology as 'social pathology'). That is, you could argue that something about the way society is organised is working against these people in some way, to the point that they are not able to manage so well and need help. This latter suggestion, then, can be seen as a critique of the social,

economic and political structure of a society. It calls into question the
organisation of society, potentially suggesting that things ought to be
organised differently so that social resources are more equally
distributed (Taylor et al., 1973).

Public drunkenness: individual problem or social illness?

Such analyses argue that defining a particular behaviour as crime
transforms how that behaviour is understood. It becomes 'human
conduct that is created by authorised agents in a politically organised
society' and used to describe 'behaviours that conflict with the interests
of the segments of the society that have the power to shape public
policy' (Quinney, 1970, pp. 15–16). The act of defining a crime is, in
part, a political act. That is, the political neutrality of criminal law is a
myth. Dutch criminologist Willem de Haan has labelled crime an
'ideological concept'. For those writers influenced by Marx, 'ideological
concepts' and the term 'ideology' can be thought about as ideas that,
whether intentionally or 'unintentionally, distort reality in a way that
justifies the prevailing distribution of power and wealth, hides society's
injustices, and thus secures uncritical allegiance to the existing social
order' (Reiman and Leighton, 2010, p. 191). While governments from
anywhere on the political spectrum can make policy and laws on the
basis of ideology, criminal law and 'how to define and respond to
crime' tend to be issues that most political parties share a consensus
about. As an ideological concept, then, de Haan argued that crime
'justifies inequality and serves to distract public attention from more
serious problems and injustices' (de Haan, 1991, p. 207).

In this context, it is worth reflecting on how many incidents (such as petty theft, shoplifting, recreational drug use, vandalism, brawls, so-called 'anti-social behaviour') that are commonly accepted as criminal would not seem to score particularly high on a scale of serious harm. And yet it is these 'minor' events that often take up much of the time and preoccupation of law-enforcement agencies and the criminal justice system (Hulsman, 1986). Conversely, the risk of suffering the crimes defined by the state as 'serious', such as murder (often referred to as intentional homicide) and armed robbery, are negligible compared to such everyday risks as workplace injury and avoidable disease (Tifft, 1994/5). Just as the risk of intentional homicide is far less than that of terminal disease or of being struck by lightning, so people are more likely to suffer accidental injury than theft (Tombs and Whyte, 2015).

Summary

- Decisions about which dangerous acts should fall under criminal law and which should not are made by those who hold the most power and privilege in society.

- Social inequality and social exclusion can be important factors to consider when thinking about what actions become prohibited by criminal law and which do not.

- There are many activities that routinely take place in society that are far more dangerous to human life and human flourishing than those traditionally defined as crimes.

3   When harms are not defined as crimes

The study of criminology involves questioning whether criminal law is working as an effective protection against the events and activities that are most harmful to individual and human flourishing.

Since the 1940s, criminologists have been considering whether a serious harm should be considered 'criminal' – that is, viewed with the same level of seriousness as those actions defined as crime – when it is not actually included as a criminal offence in the existing legal code (Sutherland, 1940, 1945). Before this time, it was largely taken for granted in academic debates that a crime had to breach criminal law, for it was assumed that criminal law would identify and categorise the most serious harms in society. For sociologist Edwin Sutherland (1940, 1945), however, the difference between harms defined as 'criminal harms' and then processed and enforced through criminal law and other harms dealt with through administrative law and other forms of regulation, was not so clear cut. Sutherland (1945) observed that the difference between those actions deemed as criminal harms and those not categorised in this way in the legal code was not necessarily related to the seriousness and harmfulness of the action or event. That is, there are serious harms in society that should, by virtue of their seriousness, be regulated by criminal law, but simply are not.

3.1   Corporate harms: lethal, but legal

A corporation is a business organisation that is registered separately from its owners. Corporations, as businesses, tend to be focused on financial balance sheets: the only costs they consider important when making decisions are economic costs (Tombs and Whyte, 2015). As a consequence, any potential social and environmental costs (or harms) that result from the operation of the corporation do not tend to be considered relevant to the owners of the corporation. Economic logic dictates that if a product sells well and makes a good profit then it should continue to be made and promoted irrespective of other considerations. One way of getting ahead in the market is to cut corners in the manufacture of products, which can mean violating basic health and safety regulations and procedures for workers or using inferior materials when making consumer goods. Due to this orientation towards profit over all other considerations, the creation of harm can be an inevitable, everyday and routine practice of the corporation (Tombs, 2015; Tombs and Whyte, 2015).

Negligence and failure to undertake rigorous testing of products or working practices because of time constraints or associated financial costs with rigorous safeguards can also generate enormous harms (Tombs and Whyte, 2015). Misrepresentation and the rushing of medical products into the market place are fuelled by the interests of making a profit. Drugs prescribed by doctors can lead to adverse reactions from patients and it is estimated that there are 'hundreds of thousands of injuries and deaths' (Freudenberg, 2016, p. 54) as a result of poorly prescribed or tested drugs. For example, in 2004 the anti-arthritis drug Vioxx was withdrawn from public consumption in the United States after evidence was released that showed that it increased the users' likelihood of having a stroke or heart attack by 50 per cent (Knox, 2004). Similar problems plagued the GlaxoSmithKline's diabetes drug Avandia, which was also withdrawn after studies found that it 'increased risk of heart attack by 43 per cent and cardiac related death by 64 per cent' (Freudenberg, 2016, p. 55). Alongside this, the pharmaceutical industry often hold patients and health services to ransom by charging high prices for drugs, or preventing the release of cheaper drugs that would be just as effective as their more expensive alternatives.

Inappropriate safeguards and cutting corners to maximise profits in the production of food can also lead to widespread social harms and health scares. Food poisoning – whether in restaurants with poor cooking practices or inexperienced, undertrained and under-pressure staff, or unhealthy animal husbandry that introduces new diseases through the food chain – can be profoundly harmful if not deadly. For public health practitioner Nicholas Freudenberg, the food, alcohol and pharmaceutical industry all:

> … use modern science and technology to seek profits in ways that harm health. They design and aggressively promote products without adequately testing their impact on health. They make false or misleading claims about the health benefits of their products and minimise the known harms or seek to obfuscate the science

that demonstrates this harm. They price unhealthy products cheaply to maximise their market penetration, but charge high prices that put healthy products out of reach of many who need them.

(2016, p. 63)

Another harm caused by corporations is air pollution (Tombs and Whyte, 2015). Airborne pollutants are linked to around 40,000 premature deaths in the UK each year (Harvey, 2018). The vast majority of air pollutants (about 70 per cent) are created through the manufacturing practices of corporate industries (Tombs and Whyte, 2015), but 'fine particulate' pollution also arises from cars and other motor vehicles. Indeed, in 2010, more people died as a result of air pollution than were killed in motor vehicle crashes (Yim and Barrett, 2012).

These lethal but legal harms of leading corporations have very serious human consequences. It is evident that the idea of what a crime is, and what is criminal, can become quite murky when wider harms and wrong-doing are also considered. Perhaps it is now becoming clearer why considering the roles power and the state play are central to thinking about 'what is crime'. They are also central to critically thinking about whether criminal law really does serve the interests of everyone in society equally.

Reflective activity: Seeing crime

What do you think about seeing the idea of crime in a broader sense, of considering the activities that usually come to mind when you think of the word crime alongside some of the harms mentioned in this section of the chapter? Does it change how you think about the idea of crime or about what is most dangerous in society?

Summary

- The study of criminology includes questioning whether criminal law is working as an effective protection against the events and activities that are most harmful to people in society.

- There is some question among criminologists whether all forms of serious harm in society should be considered as crimes or not.

- The way some corporations or industries can cause harm to people, either through the conditions under which they manufacture their products or through the harmfulness of the products themselves, provides an example that questions the way crime is defined and understood in society.

4 The Grenfell Tower fire

On 14 June 2017, a fire broke out in the 24-storey Grenfell Tower block in North Kensington, West London and burned for over 60 hours. The 2018 official number of recorded deaths of the tower-block residents was 72 (Inquest, 2018). It started after a Hotpoint fridge-freezer caught fire in one of the 127 flats in the building (BBC, 2017b).

Left: Grenfell Tower in 2011 before the cladding was added to the building; right: Grenfell Tower after the cladding had been fitted

Grenfell Tower underwent a £10 million refurbishment in 2014–16, which included extensive renovations of the bottom four floors of the building, a new heating system and major work on its exterior. The exterior modernisation largely entailed the fitting of rain-screen cladding and insulation. It is believed that around eight tonnes of cladding panels and 18 tonnes of insulation foam were attached to the tower during refurbishments (Reed and Clare, 2017). Before its refurbishment, Grenfell was constructed of 'virtually incombustible concrete' (Bowcott, 2018).

When it caught fire, it is estimated that the tower would have released '14 times more heat than a key government test allows' (Reed and Clare, 2017). The cladding's plastic core would have burned 'as quickly as petrol' (Reed and Clare, 2017), and the fire 'rose 19 storeys through the cladding in just 12 minutes' (Booth, 2018). For just an extra £5000 (safer cladding was just £2 per square metre more expensive that the sheets used), much more fire-resistant materials could have been fitted (Knapton, 2017). Grenfell Tower residents had raised concerns around the risk of fire at the tower for a number of years, but their concerns had not been addressed (BBC, 2017a).

How did so many die in the Grenfell Tower fire?

The victims of Grenfell Tower were let down on eight occasions.

A change in the law: Building regulations in London were relaxed in 1986, removing the stipulation that all external walls must have at least one hour of fire resistance to prevent flames from spreading between flats or entering inside.

Dangerous cladding: The government were warned in 2014 by fire-safety expert Arnold Turling that the gaps between the panels in the kind of cladding that was used to refurbish Grenfell Tower could become a 'wind tunnel', fanning the flames, and 'act as its own chimney', allowing the fire to spread to upper levels.

No government review: Following the deaths of six people at a similar housing block fire at Lakanal House in south London in 2009, the coroner at the inquests called for changes in regulations. There were also calls for a comprehensive inquiry into the deaths.

A single staircase: The only means of escape was from a single staircase. This also hindered firefighters. There was no legal requirement for a second staircase.

Missing sprinklers: There was no central sprinkler system at Grenfell, which members of the Fire Protection Association said would have 'undoubtedly' saved lives. Currently, sprinklers only need to be fitted up to 30 metres. However, in tall buildings, such as Grenfell Tower, it is impossible for fire hoses to reach the upper heights, leaving the top floors without any protection.

Missing fire doors: A number of doors on the 127 flats were not fire-proofed. This is in breach of existing regulations.

Inspections: The last time that Grenfell Tower was subject to a full Fire Risk Assessment was December 2015, before the changes of the refurbishments had been completed. Risk assessments should take place at least every 12 months.

Firebreaks: Under 1991 building regulations, all cladded buildings should have been controlled by 'firebreaks' – gaps in the cladding to prevent the continual burning of material – but these were absent from Grenfell Tower.

(Adapted from Knapton and Dixon, 2017)

Reflective activity: Economic or social costs?

What does the Grenfell Tower fire tell us about the focus of corporations on economic costs rather than social costs? Can the Grenfell Tower fire be considered a crime? What would be the best way to respond to the tragedy: improvements in building and housing regulations and greater priority given to health and safety, or the application of criminal law?

Summary

- The fire at Grenfell Tower in 2017 provides an example of an event that led to many avoidable deaths.

- Criminal law does not provide a straightforward way to classify the Grenfell Tower fire as a crime.

- Questioning whether criminal law is serving society well is part of the role of criminology. Events such as the Grenfell Tower fire should always lead us to ask such questions.

Conclusion

This chapter has looked at the nature and meaning of crime and processes of criminal justice, and how these can be subjected to criminological inquiry. You have investigated the definition of crime and how it relates to criminal law. You have also considered the ways in which this definition is linked to power relations and social class. The chapter also began to introduce considerations of 'harm' (specifically corporate harm), calling into question whether criminal law and criminal justice really are set up to protect the whole of society equally.

You have explored why it is important to critically question both what is included and excluded in the legal definition of crime. What the state defines as a crime does not necessarily reflect the most serious or harmful events, behaviours and actions in society but rather, can often reflect the interests of power, privilege and status. Definitions of crime are not universal and unchanging but rather alter over time, place and with regards to the people involved. Definitions of crime change as ideas about what is right and wrong in a given society change. It is essential that when thinking about what crime is that you locate your discussion within social, economic and political contexts. This is what it means to use your 'criminological imagination'.

Defining an act as a crime allows this behaviour to be dealt with by the criminal justice process. Definitions are important, then, not just in terms of how people understand something and attribute meaning, but also with regard to what people think is an appropriate and justified reaction.

References

BBC News (2017a) 'Concerns raised about Grenfell Tower "for years"', 14 June [Online]. Available at www.bbc.co.uk/news/uk-england-london-40271723 (Accessed 10 August 2018).

BBC News (2017b) 'Grenfell Tower: Fire started in Hotpoint refrigerator, say police', 23 June [Online]. Available at https://www.bbc.co.uk/news/uk-40380584 (Accessed 14 August 2018).

Booth, R. (2018) 'Grenfell firefighters deny response was affected by racism', *Guardian*, 7 June [Online]. Available at https://www.theguardian.com/uk-news/2018/jun/07/grenfell-firefighters-deny-response-was-affected-by-racism (Accessed 19 June 2018).

Bowcott, O. (2018) 'Refurbishment made Grenfell Tower a death trap, inquiry hears', *Guardian*, 5 June [Online]. Available at https://www.theguardian.com/uk-news/2018/jun/05/dangerous-building-works-turned-grenfell-tower-death-trap-inquiry (Accessed 19 June 2018).

Brighenti, A. M. (2010) 'At the wall: graffiti writers, urban territoriality, and the public domain,' *Space and Culture*, vol. 13, no. 3, pp. 315–32.

Chambliss, W. J. (1975) 'Toward a political economy of crime', *Theory and Society*, vol. 2, pp. 149–70.

Christie, N. (2004) *A Suitable Amount of Crime,* London, Routledge.

Cohen, S. (1973) 'The failures of criminology', *The Listener*, vol. 90, issue 2328, pp. 622–5.

Durkheim, E. (1895) *The Division of Labour*, London, Macmillan (this edition 2013).

Freudenberg, N. (2016) *Lethal but Legal*, Oxford, Oxford University Press.

de Haan, W. (1991) 'Abolitionism and crime control: a contradiction in terms', in Stenson, K. and Cowell, D. (eds) *The Politics of Crime Control*, London, Sage, pp. 203–18.

Harvey, F. (2018) 'Air pollution: UK government loses third court case as plans ruled "unlawful"', *Guardian*, 21 February [Online]. Available at https://www.theguardian.com/environment/2018/feb/21/high-court-rules-uk-air-pollution-plans-unlawful (Accessed 20 July 2018).

Hulsman, L. (1986) 'Critical criminology and the concept of crime', *Contemporary Crises,* vol. 10, issue 1, pp. 63–80.

Inquest (2018) 'Grenfell', *Inquest* [Online]. Available at https://www.inquest.org.uk/pages/category/grenfell (Accessed 26 September 2018).

Knapton, S. (2017) 'Grenfell Tower refurbishment used cheaper cladding and tenants accused builders of shoddy workmanship', *Telegraph,* 16 June [Online]. Available at www.telegraph.co.uk/news/2017/06/16/grenfell-tower-refurbishment-used-cheaper-cladding-tenants-accused/ (Accessed 10 August 2018).

Knapton, S. and Dixon, H. (2017) 'Eight failures that left people in Grenfell Tower at the mercy of an inferno', *Daily Telegraph,* 15 June [Online]. Available at www.telegraph.co.uk/news/2017/06/15/eight-failures-left-people-grenfell-tower-mercy-inferno/ (Accessed 10 August 2018).

Knox, R. (2004) 'Merck pulls arthritis drug Vioxx from market', *NPR,* 30 September [Online]. Available at https://www.npr.org/templates/story/story.php?storyId=4054991 (Accessed 10 August 2018).

Marx, K. and Engels, F. (1932) 'Ruling class and ruling ideas', in Storey, J. (ed.) (2008) *Cultural Theory and Popular Culture: A Reader,* 4th edn, Essex, Pearson, pp. 58–9.

Michael, J. and Adler, M. (1933) *Crime, Law and Social Science,* New York, Harcourt, Brace Jovanovich.

Quinney, R. (1970) *The Social Reality of Crime,* Boston, MA, Little Brown.

Reed, J. and Clare, S. (2017) 'Grenfell cladding "14 times combustibility limit"', *BBC News,* 19 July [Online]. Available at http://www.bbc.co.uk/news/uk-40645205 (Accessed 10 August 2018).

Reiman, J. and Leighton, P. (2010) *The Rich Get Richer and the Poor Get Prison: Ideology, Class and Criminal Justice,* 9th edn, London, Allyn & Bacon.

Scraton, P. and Chadwick, K. (1991) 'The theoretical and political priorities of critical criminology', in Stenson, K. and Cowell, D. (eds) *The Politics of Crime Control,* London, Sage, pp. 161–87.

Sutherland, E. (1940) 'White collar criminality', *American Sociological Review,* vol. 5, no. 1, pp. 1–12.

Sutherland, E. (1945) 'Is "white collar crime" crime?', *American Sociological Review,* vol. 10, no. 2, pp. 132–9.

Taylor, I., Walton, P. and Young, J. (1973) *The New Criminology,* London, Routledge and Kegan Paul.

Tifft, L. (1994/5) 'Social harm definitions of crime', *The Critical Criminologist,* vol. 6, no. 3, pp. 9–13.

Tombs, S. (2015) *Social Protection After the Crisis,* Bristol, Policy Press.

Tombs, S. and Whyte, D. (2015) *The Corporate Criminal,* London, Routledge.

Williams, K. S. (1994) *Textbook on Criminology,* 2nd edn, London, Blackstone.

Yim, S. H. and Barrett, S. R. (2012) 'Public health impacts of combustion emissions in the United Kingdom', *Environmental Science and Technology,* vol. 46, no. 8, pp. 4291–6.

Chapter 3

Law and order or harm and disorder?

by Deborah H. Drake and David Scott

Contents

Introduction

What comes into your mind when you hear the phrase 'social order'? It might be easier to think about the absence of social order, that is, disorder or a riot, when chaos breaks out. Why do you think such events happen? Sometimes social disorder can break out when there is a strong collective feeling of injustice or simply disagreement with the way things are in society. People can have very different opinions on social issues and sometimes protest against or contest changes they disagree with. (Alternatively, people may protest for changes they want to be made.) The word 'contestation' is sometimes used to describe the way that people often dispute or argue against issues, usually those that draw out strong opinions. They 'contest' these issues. So, you might say that, in some societies, gay marriage is a heavily contested social issue or that ideas about climate change are contested. It is often the case that when social disorder erupts, it indicates that there is a problem with the way society is structured or with the 'social order'. (However, just because an issue attracts wide-ranging opinions does not always mean that people will unite to collectively protest or that it will lead to social disorder.)

This chapter considers the issues of social order and contestation and why these ideas are important in criminology. But what is 'social order'? Societies have structures and systems that set out to maintain and enforce how people should (and are legally bound to) relate to one another and act. This includes formal institutions, bodies or structures, such as schools, the police, the law, regulations or codes of practice in a workplace and so on. Understanding the ways in which this 'social order' is conceived, maintained and enforced is part of what criminologists study and research, particularly when social problems arise.

The first part of this chapter draws on the 2011 English riots to consider both an example of social disorder (i.e. the riots) and how people tried to make sense of them with different — and contested — explanations. The riots were immediately defined as 'crime' in the media and by those who police and enforce criminal law. However, from the perspective of a criminologist, other ways of defining these events also needed to be considered. The second part of the chapter explores social order and contestation in a different way, highlighting how social order can be questioned when considering ideas about wider social harms, such as environmental damage. Here the concept of 'crime' itself is contested and you will begin to question the limits of criminal law.

In this chapter you will:

- consider some examples of crime and disorder and the ways in which these events were responded to

- examine the idea of the 'social contract' and how this applies to understandings of social order and disorder

- investigate competing perspectives and interests in understanding, contesting and controlling social harms.

1 Out of order: disorder and resistance

For six days, between 6 and 11 August 2011, riots broke out in several areas of London and other cities and towns in England. Thousands of people took to the streets, looting shops, vandalising banks and bank machines, damaging public property, setting fires and causing chaos. Police were sent out in large numbers to calm the disturbances. The first disturbance broke out in Tottenham, north London, following a peaceful protest over the death of Mark Duggan, who had been shot and killed by police on 4 August 2011. Violent clashes between police and the protesters erupted, leading to the destruction of police vehicles and a double-decker bus. The disturbances spread quickly to shops and residences, but also to other London boroughs and to other towns and cities, including Birmingham, Bristol, Liverpool and Nottingham.

Riot police on Upper Parliament Street after riots in Toxteth, Liverpool on 8 August 2011

There was considerable news coverage of the riots. A selection of national newspapers headlined the events by suggesting that social order had been lost and that the riots signalled chaos and anarchy.

Rule of the Mob

Daily Telegraph, 9 August, 2011

Mobs Rule as the Police Surrender the Streets

The Times, 9 August, 2011

Yob Rule

Daily Mirror, 9 August, 2011

If you read the stories that follow these headlines, you would notice that they go beyond reporting the facts. They aim to explain why the riots began, who was involved in them and what these events said about English society (or about certain individuals and groups within society). Importantly, though, these media reports were mostly based on speculation because very little was known about the root causes of the riots when the stories were written.

Reflective activity: Considering disorder

Whether or not you remember the 2011 riots, what sorts of reactions do you think that large-scale public disorder, such as rioting, tends to evoke among members of the general public, control agents (such as the police) or among the politicians in power at the time? What sorts of ideas or feelings might influence how people in each of these groups react? How would you react if this happened in your town or city? What would your first thoughts be?

As is evident in the news headlines earlier in this section, the people who were rioting were referred to as a 'mob' or, in some cases, it was assumed they were 'yobs' (suggesting it was simply groups of disaffected young men). Despite the ways in which the riots were covered in the news, public disorder on a large scale – as is the case with widespread riots – can be an indication that something is wrong in society. Such events can draw attention to the taken-for-granted agreements that maintain social order most of the time. When social disorder erupts, it can call these agreements into question. That is, perhaps certain taken-for-granted aspects of a society, such as security, equality, employment or housing, do not work for everyone in that society. To understand this point more fully, it is helpful to explore what is known as the 'social contract'.

1.1   Social disorder and the social contract

The idea of the 'social contract' is that there is an implicit agreement among everyone in a society to sacrifice some individual freedoms and to uphold some responsibilities and obligations in exchange for enjoying certain state protections and in order to live peacefully together. Underpinning the idea of a social contract are some basic assumptions about the nature of human beings and the conditions that need to be present for a society to run smoothly. However, there is some disagreement in the way different philosophers have set out these basic assumptions.

The philosopher Thomas Hobbes argued that people are motivated by their own self-interest and that they will seek pleasure and avoid pain. According to Hobbes, human beings are, in essence, engaged in a 'war of all against all' (Hobbes, 1660). However, he suggested that because they seek pleasure and avoid pain, they will tend to obey the rules of law, act reasonably and treat each other fairly or as they themselves expect to be treated. In effect, Hobbes and other philosophers, such as John Locke and Jean-Jacques Rousseau, argued that if social members want to retain the rights and privileges associated with membership of society, then they need to abide by the social contract.

Hobbes's social contract

The participants in the 2011 English riots were viewed by many news media sources as largely an opportunistic gang of people, looking for the chance to steal consumer goods and to cause damage to banks and public property just for the sake of it. This view might be in keeping with a Hobbesian approach: Hobbes might have argued that many of those who took part in these riots were, predominately, people who had 'chosen', long before the riots took place, not to undertake paid employment. As a result, they found themselves unable to access goods and services in society because in a capitalist market economy, such as the UK, access to consumer goods and services requires money. Their discontent, then, according to Hobbes, would – in effect – be a condition of their own choosing and is a result of their not participating in the economic obligations that are a part of the implicit social contract to which everyone has apparently consented.

In contrast to Hobbes and others, the philosopher, John Rawls argued that, in order for people to freely enter into the 'social contract', reasonable social and material conditions must first be present: all people must have access to the same standard of living. Once this is in place, people are in a more equal position to make choices accordingly. Only then can they decide what they might rationally want to do (Rawls, 1971). In his vision of the social contract, Rawls goes on to consider the concept of 'social justice'. Criminologist Matthew Robinson describes Rawls' view of social justice as:

> … assuring the protection of equal access to liberties, rights, and opportunities, as well as taking care of the least advantaged members of society. Thus, whether something is just or unjust depends on whether it promotes or hinders equality of access to civil liberties, human rights, opportunities for healthy and fulfilling lives, as well as whether it allocates a fair share of benefits to the least advantaged members of society.
>
> (Robinson, 2010, p. 81)

So, from Rawls's perspective, some of those who took part in the 2011 English riots may not have decided to deliberately 'opt out' of the social contract. It may have been that some people took part due to feeling excluded or constrained by the social conditions of their lives. Perhaps they were denied access to a fair share of social benefits, or not afforded opportunities to pursue healthy and fulfilling lives. That is, the widespread damage to banks and shops that took place during the riots may not have been done by people who had wilfully rejected the social contract, rather they may not have had an equal chance to participate in it.

Hobbes and Rawls offer just two philosophical perspectives that try to explain why people obey or disobey the rules of social order. To extend these discussions further, it follows that societies use a variety of strategies that aim to control, care for, exclude or protect members of society. The choice of strategies used in any society at any given point in history is influenced by a variety of factors, which need to be identified and acknowledged. This is particularly true for criminologists with an interest in agencies and agents of control, such as the police or the criminal justice system (CJS).

2   Making sense of social disorder

How close is any given society at any particular historical moment to falling into chaos and disorder? How are perceived threats to the social order defined? Who does the defining? Are some events, activities or social trends indications of potential social breakdown? Or are they just signals that something needs to change, or that some changes in society are unwelcome? How are ideas about what society 'should be' like shaped, promoted and enforced?

Students protest at the tripling of tuition fees, University of Bristol, 2010

Of course, changes in society, unexpected events, shocking crimes or so-called 'crime sprees' can all contribute to social anxiety among sections of the general public. Such events can even be seen to signal a perceived threat to society itself. However, it is not just the events themselves that can cause social unease, but is also the social reactions to them. Here, the agents and agencies of control – including the police, the voices of ruling politicians and the news media – all need to be considered too.

The explanations that circulate throughout society in the aftermath of public protests, social disorder or high-profile crimes often result from a collaboration between state agents such as the police or other security services, news media and private organisations (Ericson et al., 1991). Agents of control do not just exercise authority over people by enforcing the law or other rules of society, they also play a role in *creating social meaning* by shaping the 'official' version of the 'truth' of a situation or event. In this context of crime control, agents of the state serve two primary functions (Hall et al., 2013):

1   maintaining social order and control through enforcement and domination (i.e. handing out fines, imprisoning offenders, and delivering other forms of punishment)

2   maintaining control of the official explanation or 'truth' of a social problem.

So the shaping of the meaning of 'crime' is as much a part of social control as breaking up crowds, handing out fines or imprisoning someone.

It is important, then, to note that the news media and CJS are increasingly intermixed with each other. While the role of the police is subject to ever greater public scrutiny, especially with the widespread use of camera phones and social media, they remain an important 'official' source for interpreting the causes, and therefore the definitions, of any forms of social disorder. This is not to suggest that journalists, broadcasters and agents of control (such as the police) collude with one another to produce an inaccurate picture. Nor is it that the media are incapable of presenting views that are neutral or that do not 'spin' the story in a particular way. However, it is the case that media reporting is often grounded solely in the interpretations provided by so-called 'authoritative' sources, such as the police, the **judiciary** or politicians (Schlesinger and Tumber, 1994, p. 20). These interpretations are, in turn, dependent largely on the focused and organised police response to certain crimes (that is, the manner in which police officers enforce or ignore specific kinds of illegal behaviour when undertaking their everyday duties). This closes down the opportunity for any alternative explanations for the disorder.

Judiciary forms part of how the state upholds the law in a country. The term can be used to mean all the judges in the country's courts, whose job it is to uphold the law, but can also refer to the legal system itself.

The institutions of social control then – e.g. the police, judiciary, politicians, the media – play an active role in both the control of disorderly behaviour and how that behaviour is labelled and publicly understood. As a result, these institutions can be seen as condensed sites of power in society because they work to maintain the state's obligations in the social contract. The study of crime and criminal justice, therefore, can be a window through which to consider both the terms and conditions of the social world, and the ways in which the state may not be meeting its obligations to all members of society.

2.1   Contesting explanations of disorder

The study of social disorder enables criminologists to consider a number of broader issues about social control, regulation and the way social order is maintained. It can also draw attention to places and sites of resistance or contestation and expose dissatisfaction with the current social order.

Incidents or signals of disorder that take place in large urban centres can stimulate social anxiety about how an area is changing – particularly if there seems to be an increase of different ethnic minorities in that area or visible signs of poverty (such as increasing numbers of homeless people). Signs of disorder can be indicators that seem to mark the end of moments of relative stability. When disorder becomes visible, it may signal to some members of society that there is a social crisis afoot. (In Chapter 1, you considered how some people thought about graffiti as a sign of disorder, and considered the 'broken windows' theory that related to this.) Observing crime, disorder and policing in the context of cities can reveal much about existing social relations. This can be especially true when concepts such as 'race' or 'social class' are included in your considerations.

Some key concepts in criminology

Previous chapters have discussed certain concepts used in everyday language. A simple but useful definition of a social science concept is *a general idea or notion that tries to capture the essential features or characteristics of something*. The meaning of a concept can change over time. Some examples of social science concepts that are often used in criminology are listed here.

Race

In social sciences, 'race' is a highly contested term. The dominant social science understanding of 'race' is that it is the social interpretation of biology and culture. 'Race' is therefore viewed as social rather than biological, and so can differ in meaning from one

---

place to another, and from one period to another. (It often appears in inverted commas to indicate that its definition is influenced by the social, economic and political power relations of a culture or society at a given moment in time. In other words, it is a social construction rather than a biological reality.) It is helpful to remember that 'whiteness' is also a social construct and that racial superiority has sometimes been used to win support from poorer segments of 'white' society.

Social class

A social class is a group of people of similar status who share comparable levels of power and wealth. In social sciences, social classes are one form of social stratification or, in other words, a means by which people are categorised. Class categories can include, for example, working class, middle class and upper class.

Gender

Social science investigates the social construction of gender identities. It does not assume that gender is a natural feature of a person. There is a diversity of ideas about what it means to be 'a man' or 'a woman', but there are also experiences of gender that fall outside ideas of masculinity and femininity. Queer and transgender identities are also part of the spectrum across which people identify themselves. Within definitions of gender, there is sometimes reference to the roles, relationships and characteristics that people commonly associate with a specific gender category.

Youth

'Youth' can be defined as the time between childhood and adulthood that includes the transition from dependence to independence. The term 'youth' is often used when referring to young people in general and no specific age-group is needed.

Reflective activity: Comparing definitions

How did your own definitions of the concepts of race, class, gender and youth compare to those in the box? Had you thought about your own definitions of these concepts before and do you know where your understanding of them came from? Questioning the way you define ideas such as these is a key part of social science study.

2.2   Understanding the English riots

As you saw in Section 1, the 2011 English riots were reported by some media outlets as being perpetrated by opportunistic thieves. While we cannot know what was in the minds of everyone who participated in the riots, the way they were discussed in the media drew attention to only one way of understanding them.

A great many factors influenced why the riots started and why they spread. For example, it was argued by criminologist Tim Newburn – who conducted research about the riots in their aftermath – that the anger and conflict between community members and the police served as a flash-point (Newburn, 2015). This then set off a series of other unrelated, but similar, events and conflicts. The 'average' person arrested for taking part in the riots was:

- male

- young (aged under 25 years)

- previously known to the police

- not a gang member.

They were arrested for theft and related offences. The largest ethnic grouping arrested (according to official statistics categories) identified as 'white', closely followed by those who identified as 'black', with much smaller numbers of arrested participants identifying as 'Asian', 'mixed' or 'other' (Berman, 2014). Importantly, even though the disorder developed out of a conflict between the police and black community members, the disorder was not unquestionably driven by race-related conflicts with the police (in contrast to the 1981 Brixton riots), though it may have been a factor for many participants. There is, of course, less known about those who were involved in disorder, but were not arrested and charged. It can, however, be assumed that a number of factors came into play to contribute to the spread of the riots, including, for example, the economic downturn and the UK government's 'austerity measures' being rolled out at the time. So, it is possible that those involved in the disorder may have felt that, with cuts to services, job insecurities and falling standards of living, the government had broken the social contract.

Much of the rioting took place in or near relatively deprived, inner-city areas. The disorders involved a broad cross-section of young people and adults, but many of those involved (and who were subsequently caught) did report anti-police feelings (Lewis et al., 2011).

The factual aspects about the disorders, which subsequently came to light, include the following:

- an estimated 15,000 people were involved in the riots; about one-quarter were aged under 18 years

- by 10 August 2012, 3103 people had been tried in court: 27 per cent (846 people) were aged 10–17 years; 89 per cent were male

- two-thirds of those arrested for rioting lived in the most deprived areas in the UK.

(Muncie, 2014)

In contrast to the vast majority of media accounts of the riots, the criminologists, researchers and other critical scholars who examined them in detail have argued that inequality most likely played a significant role in why they happened. Social epidemiologists Richard Wilkinson and Kate Pickett (2012) have suggested that where high levels of inequality are present, trust and a sense of community can become weakened (Wilkinson and Pickett, 2012, p. 1). Likewise, other researchers have pointed to deprivation and social inequality (Lightowlers and Quirk, 2014) and a sense of injustice and feelings of social exclusion or isolation (Lewis et al., 2011) as being strong contributory factors to the spread of the riots.

It is evident, therefore, that there are often a variety of factors and circumstances that lead to instances of social disorder; it is rarely the case that there is a single simple explanation behind disorder. Undertaking research that takes account of different sources of information, the way stories are 'spun' in the media, and whether or not pre-existing tensions existed in a given area (or in society more generally) can help criminologists and other social scientists provide a deeper and more nuanced understanding of what an instance of social disorder may signify.

Summary

- Agents of control not only maintain order but also define how disorder is made sense of. This is because they are often the 'official' sources for interpreting the causes and definitions of any forms of social disorder that erupt.

- Signs of disorder can be indicators of deeper social unrest, conflict or contestation in society.

- Social science concepts are used to describe the social world in ways that capture a lot of information in a single word.

3   In whose interests? Social order and social harm

So far in this chapter, you have considered elements of the social order of society, but also an example of social disorder: the 2011 English riots. Social disorder is one way of contesting how the law is structured and order is maintained. Perhaps you hoped you would gain further insights into these types of events when you chose to study criminology. However, criminologists also aim to broaden the boundaries of what counts in the study of crime, disorder and control, and, in this final section of the chapter, you will consider some emerging issues in what is known as 'green criminology'. Here, the focus shifts towards an understanding of the relationship between the existing social order and social harms, and how this can shed a light upon 'contesting' the very concept of crime itself.

Workers cleaning up a chemical spill in a West Midlands lake

Green criminologists focus on the natural environment and the criminal or harmful activities that lead to environmental degradation (White, 2008). Increasingly, green criminologists have begun also to focus on the victims of environmental harm (Hall, 2013). One issue related to raising the profile and importance of attending to victims of environmental harm is that many of these harms are not defined as 'crimes'. It has been argued that:

> Many environmental disruptions are actually legal and take place with the consent of society. Classifying what is an environmental crime involves a complex balancing of communities' interest in jobs and income with ecosystem maintenance, biodiversity and sustainability.

> (Skinnider, 2011, cited in Hall, 2013, p. 219)

Environmental harms can be observed on both large and small scales, and it can often take a long time before all of the consequences of such harms are fully realised. Some examples of the way these harms are caused include:

- legal and illegal dumping of hazardous waste, which can result in death and long-term illnesses (Ruggiero and South, 2010)

- chemical exposure associated with e-waste – such as discarded mobile phones, tablets, computers – that can lead to terminal illnesses (Watts, 2010)

- contaminated drinking water, due to oil mining (United Nations Environment Programme, 2017).

Bhopal gas disaster

On 2 December 1984, an accident at the Union Carbide pesticide plant in Bhopal, India, resulted in the release of at least 40 tonnes of methyl isocyanate as well as other poisonous gases. This accident is sometimes referred to as the world's worst industrial disaster. Over 600,000 people were exposed to this toxic gas. Estimates of the death toll vary from 3800 to 16,000, but government figures suggest somewhere around 15,000 people have died as a result of this disaster. In 2017, it was estimated that around 336 tonnes of hazardous waste continued to contaminate the site of the disaster.

Surveys, including one by Amnesty International, have highlighted how toxic material still lies in heaps at the factory while survivors are fighting a losing battle to have the site cleaned up. Studies have established that people are still dying due to the poisoning of groundwater from waste leeching into three ponds as well as several sites around the factory premises … Politicians, meanwhile, are quibbling over how to address the problem. Says Rakina Khan, an activist with the Bhopal Gas Peedit Mahila Purush Sangharsh Morcha, 'Politicians are squabbling over how to clean the site, what should be done with the waste, and who should pay for it even as the pollution continues to wreak havoc and engulf more areas. For us, the people of Bhopal, even three decades later, our nightmare hasn't ended'.

(Lal, 2017)

This disaster stands as an example of why stronger industrial safety regulations need to be established and enforced. However, reluctance to implement such regulations still persists in many parts of the world.

Even though there were criminal prosecutions in the Bhopal case – eight employees, including the former Union Carbide Managing Director and Vice President, were sentenced to two years and fined US $2000 each (BBC, 2010) – criminologist Matthew Hall (2013) argues that it is difficult to address environmental harms through criminal law.

Part of the reason for this is a lack of public, political and criminal justice attention on these kinds of harms. Control agents, including police and the judiciary, are often more focused on conventional forms of crime, such as burglary, theft, or assault. Moreover, in cases when there is conflict or social activism over a particular environmental harm (such as oil spills, climate change, fracking or oil mining), agents of control are more often called in to handle the protestors, as opposed to questioning the companies that have attracted public attention in the first place. That is, the wider power and economic interests in society can sometimes be in conflict with the aims of environmental protection. Hall (citing Ebeku, 2003) points out that in Nigeria, when the economy was reliant on the oil industry:

> Nigerian judges were prioritising the country's economic reliance on the oil industry over the protection and restitution of the environment or the ordering of compensation/restitution to individual victims or to communities for the massive environmental harms caused by that industry on the Nigerian Delta.
>
> (Hall, 2013, p. 233)

As with other areas of criminology, green criminology highlights the fact that the social world and all its legal, regulatory, formal and informal structures are always made and re-made on terrain that is highly contested. Criminologist Rob White (2013) argues that there are wide differences of opinion on the tactics and strategies that can bring change to society's responses to environmental harms. From a green criminology perspective, it is important to challenge dominant power structures in society and some of the economic and social conditions that are linked to environmental degradation and destruction. Social movements and transnational activism (including organisations such as Greenpeace, Friends of the Earth, or Save the Planet) can play a vital role in mounting these challenges.

Fracking in the UK

Since the late twentieth century, there have been growing concerns that hydrocarbon drilling (oil and gas) activities accelerate global warming due to the use of fossil fuels. In some places, climate-change protestors and environmental activists have started to take direct action to thwart drilling operations, specifically, around the development of shale formation fracturing for gas (and oil), popularly known as 'fracking'. Fracking requires the hydraulic fracturing of the bedrock to release trapped natural gasses under the earth. It has been criticised for creating environment harms including:

- air pollution

- contamination of water supplies and land by the chemicals used in the fracking process

- earthquakes

- health risks for animals and humans living near to the drilling sites.

Fracking has been contested by protestors (who sometimes call themselves 'protectors') who, in the 2010s, held demonstrations at various sites in the UK where permission for drilling had been approved.

At one of these sites, Preston New Road, near Blackpool in Lancashire, protestors regularly held slow marches and sit-down protests to disrupt the daily workings of the drilling company. Protestors blocked the entrance to the drilling sites when exploratory drilling was taking place in 2017–18. The activities of the protestors were heavily policed and many local people were arrested for breaking the law.

And so this chapter, in some respects, returns to where it started – by recognising that eruptions of social disorder and unrest are not always the result of self-interested or otherwise disaffected citizens expressing their individual anger about their social circumstances. Often moments of social disorder and contestation are indications that change is underway and that different voices or issues are calling out to be addressed.

Summary

- Green criminologists focus on the natural environment and the criminal or harmful activities that lead to environmental degradation.

- One of the issues with raising the profile and importance of attending to victims of environmental harm is that many of these harms are not defined as 'crimes'.

- Like criminology more generally, green criminology draws attention to the fact that the social world and all its legal, regulatory, formal and informal structures are always made (and re-made) on terrain that is highly contested.

Conclusion

This chapter introduced the idea that the way society is structured is subject to change and contestation. The rules, laws and means of control that govern the way people live in a society can also be contested. The institutions of criminal justice – the law, the police, the judiciary – are agents of control: they exist to maintain law and order. But these institutions also act to shape how people view social conflicts. The chapter also introduced the idea of going beyond the 'taken for granted' to consider social phenomena from a more reflective standpoint, relating to ideas about the social contract and contested social relations and meanings.

Through consideration of social disorder, and specifically the 2011 English riots, the chapter showed how certain high-profile events can elicit contradictory explanations and ways of understanding such events.

Sociologist Stuart Hall and his colleagues (2013) have argued that patterns 'of crime, but also the nature of the social reaction, has a pre-history; conditions of existence' (p. 2) that are almost always omitted from the publicity, which instead concentrates on each act or event as they happen. Examining the social roots of crime and disorder, then, can help to untangle the web of social relations and the interplay between official, personal and even corporate perspectives. These perspectives converge to shape the way crime and disorder are defined, controlled and understood. Recognising this web of influences paves the way for questioning why a society may come to perceive different crimes and harms in the ways that it does. For example, some crimes or forms of disorder are described in the media or felt by the general public to be indicators that a country's way of life is crumbling around them. Other harms hardly register on the social radar.

Such questioning opens up the possibility to consider other contested issues, problems and concerns – such as those taken up in green criminology. Here, the focus shifts towards how the existing social order and power relations in society may lead to the generation of ecological harms. This may result in ordinary people engaging in social protest as a means of contesting the social order, which could involve breaking the law. Grappling with the conflicts and contestations that arise in society and the ways agents of control aim to quell these challenges to law and order (and also influence the way they are understood and responded to) is a key element of studying crime and criminal justice and is one way of developing your criminological imagination.

References

BBC (2010) 'Bhopal trial: Eight convicted over India gas disaster', *BBC News*, 7 June [Online]. Available at http://news.bbc.co.uk/1/hi/world/south_asia/8725140.stm (Accessed 13 August 2018).

Berman, G. (2014) *The August 2011 riots: a statistical summary,* House of Commons Library [Online]. Available at http://researchbriefings.parliament.uk/ResearchBriefing/Summary/SN06099#fullreport (Accessed 22 August 2018).

Ebeku, K. (2003) 'Judicial attitudes to redress for oil-related environmental damage in Nigeria', *Review of European Community and International Environmental Law*, vol. 12, no. 2, pp. 199–208.

Ericson, R., Baranek, P. and Chan, J. (1991) *Representing Order*, Buckingham, Open University Press.

Hall, M. (2013) 'Victims of environmental harms and their role in national and international justice', in Walters, R., Westerhuis, D. and Wyatt, T. (eds) *Emerging Issues in Green Criminology: Exploring Power, Justice and Harm*, Basingstoke, Palgrave, pp. 218–41.

Hall, S., Critcher, C., Jefferson, T., Clarke, J. and Roberts, B. (2013) *Policing the Crisis: Mugging, the State and Law & Order (35th anniversary edition)*, Basingstoke, Palgrave.

Hobbes, T. (1660) *Leviathan*, Oxford, Oxford University Press (this edition 2008).

Lal, N. (2017) 'Bhopal gas tragedy still haunts India,' *The Diplomat*, 19 April [Online]. Available at https://thediplomat.com/2017/04/bhopal-gas-tragedy-still-haunts-india/ (Accessed 22 August 2018).

Lewis, P., Taylor, M. and Ball, J. (2011) 'Kenneth Clarke blames English riots on a "broken penal system"', *Guardian*, 5 September [Online]. Available at www.guardian.co.uk/uk/2011/sep/05/kenneth-clarke-riots-penal-system (Accessed 22 August 2018).

Lightowlers, C. and Quirk, H. (2014) 'The 2011 English "riots": prosecutorial zeal and judicial abandon', *British Journal of Criminology*, vol. 55, no. 1, pp. 65–85.

Muncie, J. (2014) *Youth and Crime*, 4th edn, London, Sage.

Newburn, T. (2015) 'The 2011 English riots in recent historical perspective', *British Journal of Criminology*, vol. 55, no. 1, pp. 39–64.

Rawls, J. (1971) *A Theory of Justice*, London, Harvard University Press.

Robinson, M. (2010) 'Assessing criminal justice using social justice theory', *Social Justice Research*, vol. 23, no. 1, pp. 77–97.

Ruggiero, V. and South, N. (2010) 'Critical criminology and crimes against the environment,' *Critical Criminology*, vol. 18, pp. 245–50.

Schlesinger, P. and Tumber, H. (1994) *Reporting Crime*, Oxford, Oxford University Press.

United Nations Environment Programme (2017) 'UNEP Ogoniland Oil Assessment Reveals Extent of Environmental Contamination and Threats to Human Health', 7 August [Online]. Available at www.unenvironment.org/news-and-stories/story/unep-ogoniland-oil-assessment-reveals-extent-environmental-contamination-and (Accessed 22 August 2018).

Watts, H. (2010) *The Health Benefits of Tackling Climate Change*, The Lancet Health and Climate Change Series [Online]. Available at www.thelancet.com/pb/assets/raw/Lancet/stories/series/health-and-climate-change.pdf (Accessed 22 August 2018).

White, R. (2008) *Crimes against Nature: Environmental Criminology and Ecological Justice*, Cullompton, Willan.

White, R. (2013) 'The conceptual contours of green criminology', in Walters, R., Westerhuis, D. and Wyatt, T. (eds) *Emerging Issues in Green Criminology: Exploring Power, Justice and Harm*, Basingstoke, Palgrave.

Wilkinson, R. and Pickett, K. (2012) 'The poison of inequality was behind last summer's riots', *Guardian*, 5 August [Online]. Available at https://www.theguardian.com/commentisfree/2012/aug/05/riots-inequality-poverty-self-esteem (Accessed 22 August 2018).

Chapter 4
Selling the idea of crime

by Deborah H. Drake, John Muncie and David Scott

Contents

Introduction

What shapes your ideas about crime, criminals and criminal justice? Some people see law-breaking as an attack on the values and standards of society. Others see illegal acts as 'abnormal' behaviour. As earlier chapters have touched on, there are a range of activities that people view as 'inappropriate', 'deviant', 'criminal', 'wrong', 'problematic' and 'harmful'. These are often contrasted with ideas and images people have about what is 'normal'. At the very least, people expect others to adhere to social norms (the social rules and standards guiding human conduct). Yet, is crime actually *unusual conduct*, or is it, as the sociologist Émile Durkheim (1895) argued, a constant in society and a *normal social fact*? In all societies, people are expected to conform to certain rules. But people have different thresholds, values, standards and beliefs for what they view as appropriate or inappropriate conduct. Moreover, human beings are fallible and, inevitably, there are times when people break rules, including those rules that are designated as laws.

While it is important to highlight acts of inappropriate conduct and people's opinions of them, certain patterns in the ways in which human beings interact can also be identified. In terms of general interpretations of what is and what is not 'appropriate', 'deviant' or 'criminal', a general consensus on 'what people think' or 'what people want to happen' in response to a crime is often assumed (Hall et al., 1978). But where do these assumptions come from? Are such assumptions always accurate? Is there really any clear agreement about what is best to do about minor or serious crimes in a society?

This chapter considers how the media influence the social construction of crime, including 'mystifications' (Box, 1983) generated about the nature and extent of social harms. This chapter begins by dealing with the sensationalising and *overplaying* of certain illegal harms by the media, and the effects this has both on public perceptions and criminal justice policy-making. It then considers the misrepresentation or *downplaying* of the harmfulness of the legal actions of (highly profitable) consumer brands.

Thinking about which harms are underplayed and which are overplayed allows you to think critically about how the media focuses on 'what sells' (i.e. what grabs the attention of the general public). And crime sells incredibly well. In this chapter, you will dig deeper into your

Deconstructions
The questioning of how something is defined followed by thinking about it from an alternative viewpoint.

developing criminological imagination to consider how public views of crime are shaped and how such views can be interrogated. Throughout this chapter, you will subject the concepts of crime and criminal justice to a series of **deconstructions**. This process includes:

*   exploring which sources of knowledge are presented as legitimate, and which illegitimate, and how crime and its control are defined in them

*   investigating whether there are any gaps or silences in these understandings of crime.

In this chapter, you will:

*   consider some of the influences that shape public opinion and public knowledge, such as the media or other public sources of information on inappropriate conduct, crime and criminal justice

*   investigate how the media is a corporate business that, through both 'crime stories' (which are sometimes sensationalised) and the advertising of brands, is focused on profits and sales

*   explore how the power of the media, advertising and the social construction of crime is contested through the activism known as 'brandalism', which involves the subversion of messages of corporate brands.

1 News media and public opinion

When exploring how people share their ideas about crime and punishment, criminologists will often use the term 'discourse' in their writing. **'Discourse'** can be thought about simply as a pattern in written and spoken communication. It involves the way ideas are talked about (that is, if they are described, exposed, narrated or argued). One example could include the kinds of words used to describe migrants. For instance, the term 'swarm' was used by Prime Minister David Cameron to describe migrants in Calais in 2015 (*ITV News*, 2015). In the same year, controversial newspaper columnist Katie Hopkins wrote in the *Sun* that 'migrants are like cockroaches' (Hopkins, 2015). Words like this can build up a feeling about migrants as less than human and not deserving of our sympathy or support. Therefore, a discourse can include the kind of language or phrasing that is used about an individual or group and, often, who is doing the speaking or writing. So, you will sometimes see different words placed in front of 'discourse' to denote a certain category of speakers or type of communication: 'political discourse', 'academic discourse', 'media discourse' (although of course these discourses overlap, entangle, fuel and play into each other). The way different sources of information communicate ideas about crime, 'criminals' and 'criminal justice', and the language they use, can have an enormous impact on how people think about these topics, because language helps to structure thought (Wetherell et al., 2001).

Discourse
A way of describing how writing and talking are structured.

1.1 What sells?

The media – whether through the messages of advertisers, the content of news programmes, or the issues explored in highly popular soap operas – perform an important role in shaping what are thought of as the most important concerns of the day. In addition, social media and the internet are largely unregulated and increasingly perform a role in shaping what we think about, as well as the breadth of knowledge and information we are exposed to. The influence of social media (platforms such as Facebook, Instagram and Snapchat, for example), and the related idea of 'citizen journalism' (where instead of being members of an audience to the news presented by established media institutions, ordinary people start to gather and share news) began to gain popular attention in the second decade of the twenty-first century

(Wall, 2012). The role of social media and citizen journalism plays an influential role in shaping how the news is reported and framed. It remains, however, useful to refer back to older, conventional analyses of the media to understand the ways that all forms of media communications can influence people's opinions and views on current events and social issues. These analyses remain crucial to understanding how the media works.

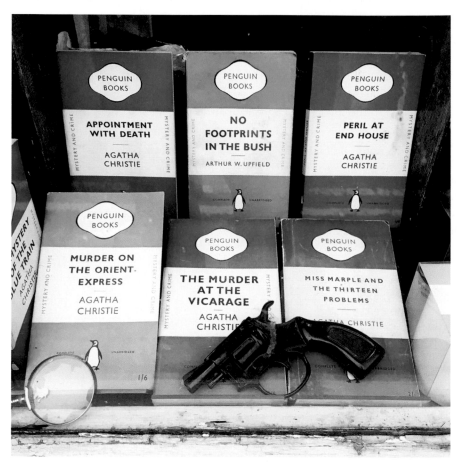

Classic crime/murder mystery books in the window of Murder and Mayhem, a second-hand bookshop in Hay-on-Wye, Wales, UK

The media can influence both our desires and our fears. But are all of the desires promoted by advertising campaigns, for example, healthy? And how are our fears shaped? Media discourse is saturated with crime. It consumes an enormous amount of media space as both entertainment and news. Whether it be TV cop shows, crime novels, docudramas, news articles, comics, blogs, videos, documentaries or 'real-life' reconstructions, crime, criminality and criminal justice appear to have an endless capacity to tap into public fear and fascination, and always have done.

Indeed, much of the publicly shared information about crime and criminal justice (and also the information we have to perceive social harms, risks and positive developments for human society) often comes via the secondary source of the media. At the same time, social media has opened up the potential for millions of people to become the generators and shapers of news (citizen journalists). You could expect, then, that the different forms of media will play a significant role in your perception and understanding of the boundaries between order and disorder, and how order is maintained.

Reflective activity: Who do you trust?

What are your main sources of information (which may have informed your knowledge and opinion) on the nature and extent of crime and the processes of criminal justice? This might include your personal experience of being a victim or an offender (or both), or sources such as social media, political speeches, and reports in the local and national press, criminal statistics or reality TV programmes.

Now ask yourself how reliable are these sources? What might be their strengths and limitations? Are there 'hierarchies of credibility' or, in other words, are some of these sources more credible than others?

1.2 Reading crime news

Since at least the mid-1880s, crime news has been a staple of the popular press. Criminologist Bob Roshier (1973) found that, between 1938 and 1967, 4 per cent of total news space was devoted to crime on average. This percentage increased significantly in the closing decades of the twentieth century. Independent researchers Paul Williams and Julie Dickinson's (1993) analysis of ten national daily newspapers in 1989 put the figure at almost 13 per cent and criminologist Robert Reiner (2007) reported that an analysis of data from the *Daily Mirror* and *The Times* between 1945 and 1991 showed a rise from an average of 8 per cent to 21 per cent. It is probably no coincidence that 'law and order' were becoming increasingly high on political agendas during this time.

But, even though the amount of crime news has increased, the type of crime reported has stayed remarkably constant. Although this type of research has declined in recent years, in the 1980s there were a number of in-depth studies of the press. For example, studies by sociologist Jason Ditton and researcher James Duffy (1983) in west Scotland and geographer Susan J. Smith (1984) in Birmingham revealed that newspapers distort the 'official' picture of crimes known to – and recorded by – the police. In west Scotland, an over-reporting of crimes involving violence and sex was noted to the extent that, during March 1981, such crimes constituted 2.4 per cent of reported incidents, yet occupied 45.8 per cent of newspaper coverage (Ditton and Duffy, 1983, p. 164). In Birmingham, personal offences such as robbery and assault accounted for less than 6 per cent of known crimes but occupied 52.7 per cent of the space devoted to crime stories (Smith, 1984, p. 290). The first research of crime news in all of the national daily newspapers in Britain in the late 1980s similarly found that newspapers regularly devoted over 60 per cent of the space given to crime reporting to stories dealing with cases of personal violence, even though they only constituted some 6 per cent of crimes reported by victims (Williams and Dickinson, 1993, p. 40).

Although newspapers do inform the public, they can also help to create a public perception that is substantially different from any 'reality' contained in victim surveys and official statistics (Smith, 1984, p. 293). Criminologist Jock Young (1974), for example, noted how the type of information that the media select and present to the public is influenced by the notion of 'newsworthiness'. He argued that, rather than providing a pure reflection of the social world, 'newspapers select events which are *atypical*, present them in a stereotypical fashion and contrast them against a backcloth of normality which is *overtypical*' (p. 241). What Young (1974) meant by this was that the media ran stories about unusual and abnormal events (such as physical violence by a stranger), which were then compared to examples of everyday life that appeared to show the opposite (such as law-abiding family life), thus obscuring hidden harms (such as domestic violence). The criminal is usually depicted as violent, immoral and a threat to an otherwise peaceful social order. This is further exacerbated in the age of social media and internet news (Roche et al., 2016).

Beware of the coverage of crime in the media!

It is not just criminologists who are concerned with the way crime is presented in the media; in some countries, services for victims train their workers to advise victims of crime directly to be mindful of the way the media presents problems of crime.

Below are some extracts from a Canadian Resource Centre for Victims of Crime web page, which focus on educating victim-service workers and victims on the way crime is covered in the media.

Understanding how the media reports crime

The media, both in the mainstream and alternative sources, such as social media and weblogs [blogs], play a large role in how members of society are informed of events that may affect them directly or indirectly.

As a victim-service worker who may be called upon to work with victims who are dealing with the media, or who may be called upon to work with the media directly, it is important to understand how the media works. While it can perform an important public service, media outlets are, first and foremost, a business. In the current global financial crisis, news media is a struggling business.

...

The media is most likely to focus on stories that highlight the unique, the sensational, the extreme, and those that have the potential to impact the greatest number of people. For crime-related stories, the media are most likely to focus on events that have occurred multiple times, for example a number of assaults or break-ins that are centred in a small geographic area, or those that are very unlikely to occur. Homicides committed by young offenders are often front-page news and may cause people to believe that youth violence is at significant levels, despite being incredibly rare. The reason they are so newsworthy is because they are so rare – they shock us, are unique and because of that, may dominate headlines for days and weeks, thereby giving the public a distorted view of how common these crimes are.

The media does not just decide what stories get that kind of attention, but what stories do not get that kind of attention. The murder of a homeless man is not likely to get as much media attention as the murder of a teenage girl from a middle-class family. The media can focus on a story, thereby making it headline news, or ignore a different story, and the public will never know.

(Canadian Resource Centre for Victims of Crime, 2018)

From these extracts, prepared to help educate those who experience crime and the people who work with them, it is evident that the distortion of crime in the news can be seen as a social problem in itself.

The media are involved in a continual search for the 'new', unusual and dramatic. This is what makes the 'news'. Professor of British Cinema Steve Chibnall (1977), has argued that press reports cannot simply be a reflection of real events because two key processes always intervene:

- selection – which aspects of events to report and which to omit

- presentation – choosing what sort of headline, language, imagery, photograph and typography to use.

It is around these processes that **news values** are structured. As Chibnall argues, the crimes most likely to receive coverage in the press are those that involve sudden injury to 'innocent others', especially in public places – in other words 'street-level' violence. Concern with such violence has typified newspaper accounts throughout the past 50 years, bolstered by such media labels as 'cosh boys', 'bullyboy skinheads', 'vandals', 'muggers', 'hooligans', 'joyriders', 'blood-crazed mobs' and 'rampaging thugs'. The concentration on these forms of crime and violence in media and public discourse does, however, reinforce limited ideas about them. Domestic violence, unsafe working conditions, pollution of the environment, corporate corruption and the regular and unhindered denial of human rights have arguably caused equal, if not more, suffering but have received less sustained press attention.

The graphic presentation of events also plays its part in constructing a particular image of crime and criminality. The drama of the story typically depends on the easy identification of opposing groups: young people versus adults; hooligans versus police; black people versus white people; 'violent' protesters and 'innocent' victims. In this way, crime is depicted in terms of a basic confrontation between the symbolic forces of good and evil. Complex social events are collapsed into simplistic questions of right and wrong. The intricate history and consequences of an event necessary to provide a fuller and more complex picture are rarely provided, or only at a later date when the terms of debate have already been firmly set (Hall et al., 1975). As a result, criminologist Yvonne Jewkes (2015) argues that 'the media is not a window on the world but is a prism subtly bending and distorting our picture of reality' (p. 288).

News values
The criteria that TV and newspaper journalists use to decide if a piece of information is, or is not, a form of news.

1.3   Consuming crime news

A story about crime, especially when singled out as significant by a senior police officer or by a judge, can 'legitimise' or make it acceptable for the press to take on a more active role.

Reflective activity: Investigating crime news reports

Think about a crime story that you may have recently read about in a newspaper (either in print or online), shared on social media, or watched in a TV news report. How much of the story did you think was just neutrally reporting the facts of the case and how much was shaped by the voice of the journalist or quotes from police or court authorities? Do you think there is a way to report on crime more neutrally? Can you see any benefits or drawbacks of doing so?

Sections of the press frequently use the opinions and concerns of those who work in the criminal process as the basis for attracting the attention of the public. Moreover, it has been argued by some media commentators that criminal justice agents and the media collude to make a significant impact on major policy decisions (Sanders and Lyon, 1995), deliberately manipulating the agenda of what people are thinking about. Other commentators (for example, Jewkes, 2015), however, highlight the importance of a coincidence of interests between the media and those who work within the criminal process. In pragmatic terms, it is not only hugely desirable for a media outlet to have an 'inside story' from an authority figure that may be considered an 'exclusive', but, at the same time, the story may also be relatively easy to produce as its content is largely shaped by the testimony of the criminal justice practitioner.

The high visibility of 'law and order' responses to crime holds certain advantages for some groups in society. Politicians, for example, often align themselves with the forces of the police and the law in order to gain public appreciation and improve their electoral chances. Crime journalists found that increasing the audience for, and profit from, crime news depends on promoting a generalised belief that law and order are breaking down. (This follows on from the success of Rupert Murdoch's sensationalist formula in the *Sun* from 1969 onwards.) Criminologist Jock Young (1974) has argued that the tendency to sensationalise the news also carries with it a tendency to amplify the phenomenon being reported. Once an incident has been identified and labelled as a 'social problem', the attention of journalists and readers tends to be directed to finding more examples of the same 'problem'. But such reporting is rarely related to an *actual* increase in such incidents at any particular time. By clustering a number of unrelated incidents under a single headline, the press create a trend, which then becomes newsworthy in its own right.

Some strong parallels have been found between media biases and public misperceptions. Using data from the 1996 British Crime Survey (which is now the *Crime Survey for England and Wales* (CSEW)), criminologists Michael Hough and Julian Roberts (1998) found that, while the national recorded crime rate fell by 8 per cent between 1993 and 1996, 96 per cent of respondents believed rates to have risen or stayed the same. When asked how much crime involves violence, 78 per cent of respondents replied 30 per cent or more, while official statistics recorded it at just 6 per cent. Indeed, while the level of crime measured by the CSEW consistently fell between the late 1990s and 2016, the CSEW has also consistently shown that, in the same period, most people believed that crime had been rising (ONS, 2017). In 2016, the Office for National Statistics (ONS, 2016) reported:

> Crime Survey for England and Wales (CSEW) showed that, for the offences it covers, there were an estimated 6.8 million incidents of crime against households and resident adults (aged 16 and over). This is a 7% decrease compared with the previous year's survey, and the lowest estimate since the CSEW began in 1981.

Nevertheless, while there may be an almost unanimous belief among criminologists that the media affects public opinion in some way, which in turn plays a part in the creation of criminal justice policy, the exact relationship between these three 'voices' (the media, public opinion and criminal justice policy) is far from clear. Although the media form a significant part of shaping this process, they are only one element. Increasingly, pressure groups, penal reform organisations and civil liberties groups have also gained access to the news media – especially through social media. They have become ever more sophisticated in designing their own media strategies to which the established law-enforcement agencies have been forced to respond. Such contradictory and alternative entries into the criminal justice policy agenda process may lead to the public querying media and official discourses.

As a result, it has been argued that while media representations do have an effect, they are unlikely to be received passively. Rather, they are interpreted by an 'active audience' as just one element in their lived experience (Livingstone, 1996; Ericson, 1991; Roshier, 1973). But this 'active audience', as sociologist Richard Osborne (1995) reminds us, increasingly lives in a media-saturated world – and this is particularly true with the rise of social media. When a primary source of 'news' is often the self-contained world of social media, facts can easily be fused with values, beliefs and myths. Crime-as-news blends into crime-as-entertainment. So, trying to isolate a specific media effect may be particularly problematic when the boundaries between drama and reality are becoming more and more blurred. By the start of the twenty-first century, this blurring had become more opaque with the denigration of any counterview to the dominant worldview as 'fake news'.

Summary

- A specific and partial view of crime is dominant in contemporary media, popular and political culture. However, it is not uncontested.

- News media are not only 'authoritative voices' of the 'facts' about the extent of crime and the effectiveness of criminal justice, but also sources of opinions about what this means for the 'state of the nation'.

- Public knowledge about crime and its control is formed by the competing voices of 'common sense', politicians, journalists, pressure groups, victims, control agents and policy-makers (and criminologists). The media, however, perform a key role in 'selling us' a particular image of what crime (and criminal harm) are in contemporary society.

2 Deconstructing crime discourses: revealing hidden harms

So far in the chapter, you have focused on the ways in which media discourses can direct public attention toward certain ways of thinking and talking about crime. In this last section of the chapter, you will consider what other kinds of messages and discourses you are bombarded with in daily life. What are some of the other ways ideas about who or what is 'good' and 'bad', 'healthy' and 'unhealthy', or 'right' and 'wrong' are communicated in society? Here you will move on from scrutinising the messages of the media and politicians, to also consider the messages of advertisers and the way global corporations play a role in constructing the social world (Klein, 2017). The discussion considers the *underplaying* or 'mystification' of the seriousness of certain harms in the media (Box, 1983).

Reflective activity: Considering brands in everyday life

In any given day, how many different brands do you buy, consume or see advertised around you? Do you notice them as brands or are many of them so familiar that you simply see them as part of the everyday landscape? Do you think that the topic of corporate brands is something that has any place in a chapter on how to deconstruct ideas about crime? Or does it seem completely off topic to you? Why do you think the chapter is now moving on to consider the messages in the advertisements of corporate brands?

2.1 Corporations and public health

The reach of corporations into the everyday lives of people all around the globe is enormous – the places people work, their form of travel, the food they eat, the leisure activities they undertake and the products they purchase are likely to have some connection to one corporation or another. The largest global corporations have enormous influence over what people think, want and believe they need (Klein, 2017). Some of the most recognisable images in modern societies around the world are the logos of food and drink brands, and top-name products include Coca-Cola and Pepsi Cola, the McDonald's Big Mac burger and the Burger King Whopper, as well as Carlsberg and Stella Artois (Klein, 1999).

A Coca-Cola advertisement in Lebanon. The Coca-Cola logo is one of the most recognised images on the planet

Brands shape our desires, wants and expectations and influence daily decisions in terms of what we decide to buy (Tombs and Whyte, 2015). But are all of the brands that people purchase good for them? Are the products most heavily advertised the best available in terms of health and well-being? Do the media accurately portray the potentially harmful consequences of such products?

An interesting debate has developed about the role of advertising and culturally desired images of the body. On the one hand, there are arguments that health problems in Western societies, such as diabetes and obesity, are increasingly linked to the consumption of certain household food and drink brands (Freudenberg, 2016). Through heavily financed advertising campaigns and highly targeted social media marketing, people, especially young adults and children, are encouraged to consume food and drink that have harmful impacts on their long-term health. According to the US paediatrician, lawyer and author David Kessler (2009) in *The End of Overeating: Taking Control of Our Insatiable Appetite*, people are often 'conditioned' through the advertising of certain brands to overeat certain kinds of food. Certain products, such as fast food and fizzy drinks, are produced and deliberately promoted as quick, easy and cheap meals. However, many of these foods and drinks contain high levels of unhealthy fats, salt, sugar and artificial flavourings and additives that have little nutritional value. Kessler argues that this can result in the 'over-consumption' of food, as people eat more to feel fuller but still fail to meet their body's nutritional requirements. It is not the availability of such foods that is necessarily the problem, it is that they are marketed so aggressively and without explicit reference to their inability to meet healthy dietary requirements. While it is worth noting that what is and is not deemed to be healthy is not universally agreed upon (Gard, 2010; Cooper, 2016; Lupton, 2016), advertising promotes certain ways of living as 'natural' in an overly simple and unproblematic way, and then exploits this imagery to promote sales of corporate brands.

Researchers at the City University of New York and the University of Michigan launched The Corporations and Health Project in 2004. The project seeks to assess the impact of corporate practices on the health of populations and to reduce the harm from these practices by influencing public policies and practices. These researchers have drawn links between corporate practices and unhealthy consumer activities. They argue:

> Industry practices that contribute to unhealthy behavior include product design, marketing (advertising, product promotion, etc.), retail distribution, and pricing. For example, the tobacco industry has targeted advertising at youth and women, increasing their smoking rates; soft drink companies establish contracts that give them exclusive rights to market their products in schools, contributing to childhood obesity; the automobile industry has heavily promoted polluting and accident-prone Sports Utility Vehicles and lobbied against stricter safety and environmental standards; and the pharmaceutical industry has promoted profitable drugs that its own research has shown to be dangerous.
>
> (Corporations and Health Watch, 2018)

As with the discussion by Freudenberg (2016) in *Lethal but Legal* that you came across in Chapter 2, these industries are contributing to a social world that is less safe, harmonious and risk-free, even though they are completely legal. The influences these industries have in the social world is, in part, related to the power they have to construct themselves as good, legitimate and even fun. The kind of advertising they tend to use is concerned with:

> Not the taste, but the brand image, reinforcing food marketers' practice of emphasising image over substance, and fantasy over health-related attributes. This leads to the foundation of 'brand communities' (groups of people whose identity is linked to their brand preferences). By appealing to these identities, advertisers make consumers feel that by using a product they can overcome feelings of isolation and loneliness.
>
> (Freudenberg, 2016, p. 13)

Reflective activity: Questioning adverts

Are there any ways to start to question the authority, legitimacy or strength of powerful corporate advertisers, who may not have the best interests of the general public at the forefront of their corporate strategy, when they are seeking to sell their products?

2.2   Deconstructing advertising: 'subvertising' and 'Brandalists'

In an effort to counter the widespread dominance of mainstream media and advertising of unhealthy consumer products, a grass-roots movement of resistance has been gaining momentum. 'Subvertising' is the process of creating spoof versions of real adverts in order to subvert them. This highlights how the original adverts by corporations may be damaging to public health by promoting products and lifestyles that are either damaging human well-being or the environment.

Advertising billboards and posters are not only both legal and morally acceptable in wider society, but also expected and, often, enjoyed as a form of art or entertainment. Yet, advertising may perform a key role in directing attentions away from certain kinds of crime or, at the very least, perpetuating particular social harms. Returning briefly to the issue of graffiti, which you examined in Chapter 1, you may have noticed several similarities between acts of graffiti and billboard and poster advertising. Both graffiti and advertising:

- take place in public spaces

- are imposed upon walls and other objects

- are intended for strangers and passers-by

- have a message of some kind they wish to get across

- may be artistic in merit (or not)

- may wish to elicit some kind of response from their social audience

- may be unwelcome by certain people who view them.

The key difference is that one is legal, well-financed and professionally organised, often by a corporation, while the other is illegal, does not generally have any financial inducements and is the creation of a specific individual or group.

Both advertising and graffiti can be seen as symbolic: advertising is symbolic of the power of corporate interests, albeit sometimes under the guise or with the purpose of benefiting the consumer; graffiti is symbolic of a self-conscious form of resistance seeking to challenge the ownership and control of public space. What is certain is that they are both about power and communication, with advertising intending to influence decisions on what products people buy and with (at least some) graffiti artists intending to express a counter-narrative that all is not well in society.

Subvertising, then, aims to subvert the message of advertising, and expose the benefits that the corporation advertising the product gains from social inequalities. This can involve adding a different message and presenting it by reusing the original logos and design of the corporate advert. Banksy, whom you encountered in Chapter 1, has this to say about the process:

> Any advert in a public space that gives you no choice whether you see it or not is yours. It's yours to take, re-arrange and re-use. You can do whatever you like with it … Asking for permission is like asking to keep a rock someone just threw at your head. … You owe the companies nothing. Less than nothing, you especially don't owe them any courtesy. They owe you. They have re-arranged the world to put themselves in front of you. They never asked for your permission, don't even start asking for theirs.
>
> (Banksy, 2012)

The subvertising group 'Brandalism' installed more than 600 subverts around the streets of Paris critiquing corporate sponsorship of the 2015 United Nations Climate Change Conference. Sponsors included Volkswagen, just months after their emissions scandal had broken

'Brandalism' is a subvertising movement based in the UK. As subvertisers, Brandalism often subverts the original and intended symbolic message of an advertisement.

> Brandalism is an international street art collective that subverts advertising in urban space. We mobilise artists around the world to take creative action against ads as together we imagine a world beyond consumerism. Why advertising? Alongside corporate lobbying, it is one arm of multinational corporate power fuelling the distractive and destructive forces of consumerism. With nothing more than high-vis jackets, special keys, and shared creative principles we create the world's largest ad takeovers. We exist to agitate, educate, and facilitate those who want to reclaim public space from corporate control.

> (Brandalism, 2018)

Examples of Brandalist work in the UK include the 2012 subvertising campaign, which involved hijacking 35 billboards across Leeds, Manchester, Birmingham, Bristol and London.

Another sponsor of the United Nations Climate Change Conference was Air France, who the Brandalism activists felt were actively contributing to global warming through their consumption of fossil fuels

We seek to challenge the destructive impacts of the advertising industry and tackle its detrimental impact on issues such as body image, consumerism and debt. The advertising industry creates pressure when they manipulate our needs and desires. Pressure to have the latest gear, clothes and phones. This pressure erupted when kids took to the streets across the country to claim what they had been told that they needed. We're lab rats for ad execs who exploit our fears and insecurities through consumerism. I'm a human being, not a consumer. So by taking these billboards, we are taking these spaces back. If Sao Paolo in Brazil can ban all outdoor advertising, so can we.

(Brandalist Campaigner (Battersby, 2012))

In 2016, a further group of Brandalists targeted the London Underground as part of their campaign to have outdoor advertising banned. The Brandalists called themselves the 'Special Patrol Group', which itself is a subversion: the term was originally used in the 1980s to describe specialist police officers. The Brandalist Special Patrol Group describe advertising as a form of 'visual pollution that is harmful for the public' (Anonymous, 2018, p. 19) and altered 400 adverts on the London Underground with subverts, including poster subverts that announced that 'Advertising shits in your head' (Anonymous, 2018). In response to the campaign, a Transport for London spokeswoman is reported as saying: 'This is not an authorised advert. It is fly-posting and therefore an act of vandalism, which we take extremely seriously' (cited in Grafton-Green, 2016).

Subvertising is one way of highlighting how the media perform a central role in the social construction of crime. By highlighting harms that are not illegal, Brandalists and other subvertisers shine a spotlight on how the media are influenced by the profit motive. Subvertising is a strategy that has been deployed in a variety of campaigns – such as the feminist resistance to the 'beach body ready' Protein World adverts in 2015, which suggested that only slim women should wear bikinis (Sanghani, 2015). While the activities of subvertisers may well be portrayed as a form of 'ideological vandalism' (Cohen, 1973), it is also a morally and politically significant form of activism. It is intended to stir our criminological imaginations about the meaning and application of the label 'criminal' and to help create greater acknowledgement of the nature and extent of legal social harms in the contemporary world (Cohen, 2001).

Summary

- Criminologists argue that there is an underplaying of the harms caused by corporate interests and that advertising is guided solely by financial costs at the expense of social costs.

- A discussion of social harms can disrupt taken-for-granted and 'common-sense' assumptions about the nature and definition of crime.

- Subvertising is a form of activism that changes adverts to illuminate the harms of corporate brands, and highlights the need for changes in the law regarding public advertising.

Conclusion

The media perform an important role in shaping what is thought about as a problem and how it should best be responded to. This chapter explored how crime discourses in the media both underplay and overplay certain social harms, and how this can influence 'common-sense' understandings of crime. It questioned the over-reporting of crime stories based on specific 'newsworthy' criteria, which sensationalise interpersonal physical violence in public spaces, while at the same time under-reporting other potentially lethal harms (Box, 1983). This deconstruction of crime discourses led to a consideration of the role of corporations and the pursuit of profit in the social construction of illegal harms. In so doing, it raised questions about whose interests are being served by media crime discourses.

At the same time, the role of corporate advertisers in shaping what is desired and what is harmful was also questioned. The promotion of corporate brands in the media was revealed as being based on the accumulation of financial profit rather than human well-being, health and global sustainability. Subvertisers expose the hidden agenda of global corporations and also the potentially harmful nature of the products that are being sold. In so doing, they provide an excellent illustration of the 'deconstruction' of media messages about crime and social harm.

References

Anonymous (2018) *Advertising Shits in Your Head: Strategies for Resistance,* London, Dog Section Press.

Banksy (2012) 'Letter on advertising', *Genius* [Online]. Available at https://genius.com/Banksy-letter-on-advertising-annotated (Accessed 4 September 2018).

Battersby, M. (2012) 'Brandalism: street artists hijack billboards for "subvertising campaign"', *Independent,* 17 July [Online]. Available at www.independent.co.uk/arts-entertainment/art/features/brandalism-street-artists-hijack-billboards-for-subvertising-campaign-7953151.html (Accessed 19 September 2018).

Box, S. (1983) *Crime, Power and Mystification,* London, Routledge.

Brandalism (2018) *Brandalism* [Online]. Available at http://brandalism.ch (Accessed 8 January 2018).

Canadian Resource Centre for Victims of Crime (2018) 'Understanding how the media reports crime' [Online]. Available at https://crcvc.ca/publications/media-guide/understanding/ (Accessed 4 August 2018).

Chibnall, S. (1977) *Law and Order News*, London, Tavistock.

Cohen, S. (1973) 'Vandalism', in Ward, C. (ed.) *Vandalism*, New York, NY, Van Nostrand Reinhold.

Cohen, S, (2001) *States of Denial*, Cambridge, Polity Press.

Cooper, C (2016) *Fat Activism: a Radical Social Movement*, Bristol, HammerOn Press

Corporations and Health Watch (2018) 'Overview' [Online]. Available at www.corporationsandhealth.org/about-us/overview/ (Accessed 4 September 2018).

Ditton, J. and Duffy, J. (1983) 'Bias in the newspaper reporting of crime news', *British Journal of Criminology*, vol. 23, no. 2, pp. 159–65.

Durkheim, É. (1895) *The Rules of Sociological Method and Selected Texts on Sociology and its Method,* New York, The Free Press (this edition 1982).

Ericson, R. (1991) 'Mass media, crime, law and justice', *British Journal of Criminology*, vol. 31, no. 3, pp. 219–49.

Freudenberg, N. (2016) *Lethal but Legal,* Oxford, Oxford University Press.

Gard, M. (2010) *End of the Obesity Epidemic*, London, Routledge.

Grafton-Green, P. (2016) 'Tube network covered with anti-advertising messages by "brandalism" group', *Evening Standard*, 14 November [Online]. Available at https://www.standard.co.uk/news/transport/tube-network-covered-with-antiadvertising-messages-by-brandalism-group-a3395291.html (Accessed 19 September 2018).

Hall, S., Clarke, J., Critcher, C., Jefferson, T. and Roberts, B. (1975) *Newsmaking and Crime*, Birmingham, Centre for Contemporary Cultural Studies.

Hall, S., Critcher, C., Clarke, J., Jefferson, T. and Roberts, B. (1978) *Policing The Crisis: Mugging, the State, and Law and Order,* London, Macmillan.

Hopkins, K. (2015) 'Rescue bats? I'd use gunships to stop migrants', *Sun*, 17 April, p. 11.

Hough, M. and Roberts, J. (1998) *Attitudes to Punishment,* Home Office Research Study No. 179, London, HMSO.

ITV News (2015) ITV, 30 July.

Jewkes, Y. (2015) *Media and Crime*, 3rd edn, London, Sage.

Kessler, D. (2009) *The End of Overeating: Taking Control of Our Insatiable Appetite*, London, Penguin.

Klein, N. (1999) *No Logo: Taking Aim at the Brand Bullies*, Ottowa, Knopf Canada.

Klein, N. (2017) *No is Not Enough,* London, Blackstone Publishing.

Livingstone, S. (1996) 'On the continuing problem of media effects', in Curran, J. and Gurevitch, M. (eds) *Mass Media and Society*, London, Arnold, pp. 305–24.

Lupton, D. (2016) 'Explainer: what is fat studies', *The Conversation*, 21 September [Online]. Available at https://theconversation.com/explainer-what-is-fat-studies-63108 (Accessed 19 September 2018).

Office for National Statistics (ONS) (2016) *Crime in England and Wales: Year Ending March 2015* [Online]. Available at https://www.ons.gov.uk/peoplepopulationandcommunity/crimeandjustice/bulletins/crimeinenglandandwales/2015-07-16 (Accessed 19 September 2018).

Office for National Statistics (ONS) (2017) *Public Perceptions of Crime in England and Wales: Year Ending March 2016* [Online]. Available at https://www.ons.gov.uk/releases/publicperceptionsofcrimeinenglandandwales (Accessed 19 September 2018).

Osborne, R. (1995) 'Crime and the media: from media studies to postmodernism', in Kidd-Hewitt, D. and Osborne, R. (eds) *Crime and the Media: The Post-Modern Spectacle*, London, Pluto, pp. 25–49.

Reiner, R. (2007) 'Media made criminality: the representation of crime in the mass media', in Maguire, M., Morgan, R. and Reiner, R. (eds) *The Oxford Handbook of Criminology*, 4th edn, Oxford University Press, Oxford, pp. 302–40.

Roche, S. P., Pickett, J. T. and Gertz, M. (2016) 'The scary world of online news? Internet news exposure and public attitudes toward crime and justice', *Journal of Quantitative Criminology*, vol. 32, no. 2, pp. 215–36.

Roshier, B. (1973) 'The selection of crime news by the press', in Cohen, S. and Young, J. (eds) *The Manufacture of News Social Problems, Deviance and the Mass Media*, London, Constable.

Sanders, C. R. and Lyon, E. (1995) 'Repetitive retribution: media images and the cultural construction of criminal justice', in Ferrell, J. and Sanders, C. (eds) *Cultural Criminology*, Boston, NE University Press, pp. 25–44.

Sanghani, R. (2015) '"Are you beach body ready?" Feminists deface "body-shaming" ad', *Telegraph,* 27 April [Online]. Available at https://www.telegraph.co.uk/women/womens-life/11565200/Protein-World-beach-body-ready-ad-vandalised-by-women-for-body-shaming.html (Accessed 19 September 2018).

Smith, S. (1984) 'Crime in the News', *British Journal of Criminology*, vol. 24, no. 3, pp. 289–95.

Tombs, S. and Whyte, D. (2015) *The Corporate Criminal. Why Corporations Must Be Abolished. Key Ideas in Criminology,* Abingdon, Routledge.

Wall, M. (2012) *Citizen Journalism: Valuable, Useless or Dangerous,* London, International Debate Education Association.

Wetherell, M., Taylor, S. and Yates, S. J. (2001) *Discourse Theory and Practice: A Reader,* Milton Keynes, Open University Press / London, Sage Publications.

Williams, P. and Dickinson, J. (1993) 'Fear of crime, read all about it', *British Journal of Criminology*, vol. 33, no. 1, pp. 33–56.

Young, J. (1974) 'Mass media, drugs and deviance', in Rock, P. and Mackintosh, M. (eds) *Deviance and Social Control*, London, Tavistock, pp. 229–59.

Block 2:
Defining crime

Chapter 5

The murder puzzle: intentional homicide, avoidable deaths and social murder

by Deborah H. Drake and David Scott

Contents

Introduction

You might think that one of the most likely ways someone will die 'prematurely' is when they are murdered. The media provide society with regular accounts of murder, violent death and serial killers.

A collage of sensationalist newspaper headlines reporting on various crimes

It is, perhaps, no coincidence that newspapers cover stories about murder, crime and mayhem in ways that are eye-catching, shocking and provocative. Crime fiction and true-crime stories in film and television are among the highest grossing genres – people seem to love 'a good murder'. Perhaps this is because although, at a distance, murder is a fascinating and captivating event, it is something that no one would ever want to happen to them or anyone they love. When a 'real-life' murder is committed, people often become entranced and fully absorbed in its details, perhaps because they are afraid of it happening to them and they want to know that everything is being done to prevent it from happening again. Despite the intrigue and interest that people may have in murder, it is an unlikely event.

If you think about, or classify, murder as an avoidable death and compare it to other causes of premature death that are completely avoidable, an interesting – and somewhat sobering – picture emerges. In the UK, there are a variety of causes of premature death that are far more likely than murder. In 2016/17, 723 people were murdered (Statistica, 2017), but:

- in 2015, 6639 people committed suicide (Samaritans, 2017)

- in 2016, 1792 people were killed in fatal road traffic incidents (Department for Transport, 2017)

- the deaths of an estimated 12,000 people from lung disease every year are linked to past exposures to harmful substances in working environments (Health and Safety Executive, 2017a).

Comparing these statistics is not to say that any of these causes of death are more or less serious than any other. The end result, the loss of a human life, is equally tragic regardless of the circumstances. What is worth thinking about, however, is the relative importance that is given by society to the different causes of death, and which avoidable deaths come under the remit of criminal law and which do not. Thinking about how, and under what circumstances, criminal law is applied is a key issue for criminology.

Different countries and legal jurisdictions have different strict definitions for murder, manslaughter, and homicide. The act of murder can also be referred to as intentional homicide and is defined by the United Nations Office on Drugs and Crime (UNODC) as an 'unlawful death purposefully inflicted on a person by another person' (2013, p. 9). To avoid becoming caught up in the different legal technicalities of these different definitions and to help you to focus only on the problem of unlawful and lawful deaths, as opposed to differing legal definitions of these terms, this chapter will use the terms 'murder' and 'intentional homicide' (as defined above) interchangeably.

This chapter will explore whether certain avoidable deaths should be separately classified as intentional homicides. You will consider this as a 'murder puzzle', asking 'Should this death be thought about as murder?', as you consider circumstances in which different avoidable deaths happen. As you will note, criminologists have come to different conclusions about how to define the problem of avoidable deaths, the way different harms are prioritised in society, and how blame and responsibility are applied. This chapter introduces you to this debate.

In this chapter you will:

- consider the ways different avoidable deaths are defined
- examine the ways social inequalities influence how different causes of premature death are defined in society
- explore different ways of allocating blame/social responsibility.

Avoidable Deaths   Natural Deaths

Premature Deaths   Lawful Deaths.

Unlawful Deaths

Murder, Manslaughter, intensional homicide

Murder = intensional homicide

✗ But How & who decides if
A death = Murder (homicide) ?

The Power to criminalise
The Power to de criminalise
The Power to prevent criminalisation

✗ Power to define a death(s) as Murder (s)
and vis-versa!

1   Exploring the problem of intentional homicide

Have you ever thought about how different actions or activities become defined as illegal in criminal law? Or why some activities are viewed as crimes in one country, but not in another? Did you know, for example, that in the United States it is legal for almost anyone to carry a gun, provided that certain legal restrictions are followed? However, the sale of Kinder Surprise – a popular children's chocolate treat in many countries around the world – is illegal there on the basis that they contain a non-food item inside a food item, and thus could lead to a child choking.

A Kinder Surprise, showing the toy inside the chocolate egg

'Moms Demand Action' is a pressure group in the United States that lobbies against gun violence in the interests of child safety. Their 'Kinder Surprise' campaign (Moms Demand Action, 2013) uses the banning of these chocolate eggs as a means of gaining perspective, citing that 3000 children a year are killed by guns and yet between Kinder Surprise and guns, only the Kinder Surprise is banned. Campaigns such as these are sometimes a means by which laws are changed. At the time of writing, however, this particular campaign has not been successful.

Governments set out laws as societal rules that aim to prevent people and social groups from engaging in certain activities. Laws are intended to promote general safety and protect the individual rights of citizens against abuses by other people in society, by corporations, or even by the government itself. Every country has its own laws to govern what is deemed to be acceptable or unacceptable in that society. Few laws are universal or common to every society around the world. The one law that can be found in many countries, though, is the law against the intentional killing of another person.

1.1   Variations in intentional homicide rates

To investigate how widespread the problem of intentional homicide is, it is helpful to look at variations between and within countries.

Reflective activity: Comparing international crime rates

Have you ever thought about how crimes are recorded and compared across different countries? Do you think it would be straightforward to compare crime rates between different jurisdictions – aren't acts such as assault, burglary or robbery relatively easy to count and compare? Well, it turns out they are not and comparing crime rates between different countries is nearly impossible. This is because legal jurisdictions differ in the way they define individual crimes and, moreover, even different law-enforcement agencies within a given legal jurisdiction might record crimes differently. For example, some law-enforcement agencies record 'all reported' crimes in their final figures, while others may only record 'proven and solved' crimes.

All is not lost, however, for those wishing to compare international crime rates. Intentional homicide is one of the crimes that is most effectively and consistently recorded by law enforcement across and within legal jurisdictions. As a result, intentional homicide rates are often used for international comparison as a proxy for levels of violent crime, and sometimes even overall crime rates (Malby, 2010).

Do you think the general risk of harm or death in a given society is indicated by the number of homicides in that society?

What factors might you consider when trying to answer this question?

The graph in Figure 5.1 includes figures of intentional homicide rates per 100,000 people from selected countries around the world. It reveals patterns in these rates, with some countries and parts of the world showing generally higher rates in comparison to other parts of the world. It is evident that certain parts of Central and South America (such as Honduras, El Salvador and Venezuela), for instance, have high rates of intentional homicide, whereas Japan, Sweden and the UK have the lowest. If all individuals around the world were equally likely or unlikely to engage in an act of intentional homicide, then one might expect that all countries would reveal a broadly similar pattern of intentional homicide rates. That is, if 'human nature' and individual characteristics alone accounted for the reasons why people commit a murder, then a much more similar picture of murder rates around the world would be expected. This is because there is no evidence that individuals from particular places or cultural backgrounds are more or less likely to commit homicide. Instead, what is revealed is a picture that is clearly associated with geography. What might account for such high rates of intentional homicide in particular places?

Social trend
is a term often used in sociology and can refer to social patterns that can be measured statistically or social activities that have mass appeal.

When social scientists and, in particular, criminologists, try to look for the reasons behind why certain social patterns emerge, they often look for other **social trends** or indicators by examining measurable data on the economic or political picture of a country. It is worth noting that the countries with the highest levels of intentional homicide (as presented in Figure 5.1) are also societies that, generally speaking, also have high levels of social and economic inequality. Indeed, according to measures of inequality, some of the regions of Central and South America are among the most unequal in the world (Bárcena Ibarra and Byanyima, 2016).

Moreover, it is also important to look at inequalities within societies. In Figure 5.1, you will note that among countries from the comparatively more economically advantaged West – the United States, UK, Sweden, Canada – the United States, the richest country in the world, has the highest intentional homicide rate. One of the factors that may explain this is that the United States is a country with relatively high levels of inequality – that is, a larger gap between the rich and the poor. Even though the intentional homicide rates shown and discussed above are concerning in and of themselves, the potential link between intentional homicide rates and inequalities means that there are deeper social issues and problems that also need to be studied and considered.

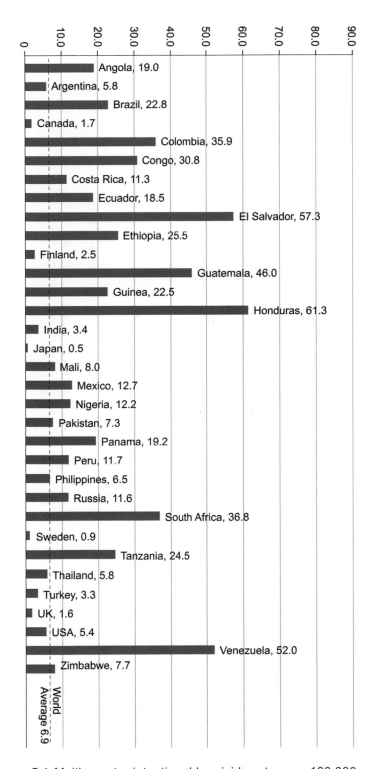

Figure 5.1 Multi-country intentional homicide rates per 100,000 people

Summary

- Intentional homicide rates vary considerably, depending on where you live in the world.

- There appears to be a link between intentional homicide and inequality.

2 Intentional homicide and inequality

For UK-based social geographer Danny Dorling, murder statistics are a reflection of social and economic inequalities. He drew on data on poverty, where people live, and the likelihood of intentional homicide to examine if there is a link between inequality and death by murder. According to Dorling, 'the poorer the place you live, the more likely you are to be murdered' (2005, p. 184).

A number of other researchers (Marmot, 2004; Wilkinson and Pickett, 2010) have also found that the poorest neighbourhoods have the highest intentional homicide rates. Inequality and risk of intentional homicide appear to be intimately related (Wilson and Daly, 1997). It is implied from this data that, in an unequal society with high levels of status competition, the social standing of a person and where they live can have an enormous impact on the likelihood of them being the victim of an intentional homicide.

The relationship between inequality and intentional homicide, however, is not as clear- cut as it first seems. There are variations within the UK and ever-changing long-term trends of both inequality and intentional homicide rates. Overall, inequality has remained relatively stable in the UK from 1990 to 2016, although this does not mean it is an 'equal' society, it just means that levels of inequality have not narrowed or widened very much in this time period (Equality Trust, 2016). Intentional homicide rates, however, have fluctuated somewhat. For example, in England and Wales, incidents of intentional homicide generally increased from the 1960s up until the early 2000s, but there was then a downward trend to the year ending March 2015 (Office for National Statistics, 2017). However, in 2015 there were 576 recorded intentional homicides, but 697 in 2016, an increase of 21 per cent (BBC News, 2017). By contrast, in Scotland in 2015/16 to 2016/17, there was an overall rise in intentional homicide from 58 to 61, a 5 per cent increase (Scottish Government, 2017).

The longer term trend in Scotland is one of decline. In 2014–15, there were 59 recorded intentional homicides in Scotland, the lowest number since 1976 (Skott, 2015, pp. 37–8). Furthermore, over the ten-year period from 2007/08 to 2016/17, the number of intentional homicides fell from 115 (in 2007/08) to 61 (in 2016/17), a drop of 47 per cent (Scottish Government, 2017). Such data indicates that national and international homicide statistics need careful thinking about and are not always a straightforward indicator of other social trends. However, the intentional homicide data in the UK (2007–17), broadly speaking, conforms with Dorling's (2005) broader contextual point that people who live in impoverished areas are more likely to be victims of intentional homicide than those who live in wealthy areas.

2.1   Inequality and premature death

International differences in intentional homicide rates can offer clues as to the social conditions in which intentional homicides are more likely to occur. Similarly, a well-established way of exploring the impact of economic inequalities on premature mortality (a term used to describe early death rates) is by looking at differences in mortality rates between different countries or regional areas.

Life expectancy for men and women in the least wealthy nations are generally much lower than those in the wealthiest nations. In 2016, Sierra Leone had the world's lowest life expectancy, with women expected to live on average 50.8 years and men only 49.3 years. Although life expectancy in Algeria in North Africa is 75.6 years, life expectancy for men and women in a number of other African countries, such as Nigeria, are as low as 50 years. This can be compared to countries such as the United States, Sweden, UK and Japan where people are, on average, expected to live to 75 years, which is at least 25 years longer, or half as long again. Of course, all of the countries named above have very different economic and political climates and all have variations within them, with some regions having higher life expectancies than others. However, broadly speaking, the reason why so many people die at relatively young ages in unequal or poorer societies is because social conditions, including access to clean water and sanitation, are inadequate. By contrast, improvements in public health and meeting basic everyday human needs for shelter, food and warmth all increase life expectancy.

As suggested above, differences in how long people live are not just restricted to whether someone lives in a rich or poor country, differences are also found within populations of the same country (Dorling, 2005). It is not just how much or how little a person has in terms of their income, but also how they compare in relative terms against comparisons with other people. In other words, the problem is not just poverty but, once again, social and economic inequality. What is important for health and wellbeing is where people are positioned in the **social hierarchy** – the higher up you are on the social ladder, the healthier you are likely to be. Every step down the social ladder leads to a deterioration in health. Rather than being simply a reflection of a divide between the rich and the poor, health inequalities operate across a gradient or sliding scale that directly reflects status and class (Marmot, 2004; Wilkinson and Pickett, 2010). Differences in health/ill-health reflect the way a society is organised and the nature and extent of inequalities (Bambra, 2016). This means that even overall wealthy countries can have high levels of inequality and, consequently, a lower life expectancy for those who live in the poorest areas.

In 2016, the UK had the largest gap between rich and poor in Europe: the richest 20 per cent were seven times richer than the bottom 20 per cent (Bambra, 2016). In 2017, the richest 100 people in the UK had combined assets of over £300 billion, which is more than 10 times the combined assets of the poorest 20 per cent of the population (around £28 billion). Perhaps unsurprisingly, people who are rich generally live a lot longer than people who are poor. The difference can be as great as 20 years (Marmot, 2015).

Social hierarchy entails the classification of people into different ranks according to social, economic or ideological criteria. The ranking system operates like a ladder, with one category of people placed higher than the other(s) in terms of status, respect, value and worth.

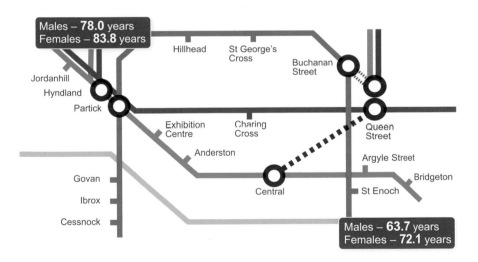

Figure 5.2 Inequalities in life expectancy in Glasgow (2015)

The map in Figure 5.2 shows health inequalities in areas of Glasgow. It shows that when travelling from Jordanhill (a wealthy area in the West End of Glasgow) to Bridgeton (on the less well-off East End), life expectancy for males goes down by two years for every station on the train line. On average, then, a man born in Bridgeton can expect to live 14.3 years less than if he were born in Jordanhill, and a woman 11.7 years less (NHS Scotland, 2017).

The interesting question that the links between intentional homicide and inequalities poses is whether there are other causes of premature death that should be receiving greater political and social attention than intentional homicide. This is the 'murder puzzle' that has been set out by Dorling (2005): should the harm and injury of intentional homicides be located within a broader context of avoidable deaths/mortality rates? Should intentional homicides be recognised, among other avoidable deaths, as a side effect of the social and economic dangers of inequality?

Summary

- Less equal societies have higher intentional homicide rates.

- The likelihood of intentional homicide and other forms of premature death varies within countries, according to where you live.

- There is a link between inequality and life expectancy.

- The 'murder puzzle' for criminologists is whether it is helpful to separate unlawful killings and intentional homicide from other forms of avoidable deaths.

3 Taking account of other avoidable deaths

The taking of a human life is generally viewed as the most serious form of harm a person can inflict or experience. However, it is clear that studying the problem of intentional homicide is not easy and, in fact, suggests that intentional homicide may be an indicator of other social ills. These include other harms, such as avoidable deaths, that also need further consideration. Part of the reason why there is difficulty in recognising a fuller range of harmful and deadly activities in society is that only certain events and acts are taken up through criminal law. Defining 'what is a crime' on the most basic of levels, depends on the legal code or formal laws of a given country or jurisdiction. However, some criminologists question whether criminal law is accurately or effectively identifying the most serious harms in society.

3.1 Criminal harm and other avoidable deaths

When should an avoidable death be defined as intentional homicide? This depends on whether the death meets the criteria of criminal law in a given country and is, therefore, defined as a *'criminal* harm'. In other words, a 'criminal harm' is any harmful act that has been defined as illegal within criminal law. The definition of 'intentional homicide' by the UNODC, used in the Introduction of this chapter, states that it is 'the unlawful death purposefully inflicted on a person by another person' (2013, p. 9). Implicit in this definition is the idea of intention – the planned goal of *purposefully* inflicting death on another person. As the definition also includes the requirement that the death is 'unlawful', 'criminal blame' also implicitly plays a role in this definition. 'Criminal blame' is the idea that an individual or group of people is responsible or *culpable* for the illegal act or harm which has taken place. Intentional homicide is often clearly defined in a country's criminal law code and it is the law that sets the criteria upon which a death is deemed to be lawful or unlawful, and thus how blame and responsibility are to be allocated. However, criminologists have argued that the law is not the only means by which the harm and responsibility for avoidable deaths could be recognised and acknowledged.

There are many other avoidable deaths that are more common-place than intentional homicide. It is only through questioning the assumptions on which criminal laws are based that different ways of thinking about the harms that threaten human life can be better understood. This criminological approach draws upon what has been called the 'criminological imagination' (Young, 2010), and it involves examining how social and economic circumstances influence the social world, the choices people make, and the meanings and motivations that drive them (Taylor, Walton and Young, 1973).

Reflective activity: Is it murder, is it a crime?

Consider the list below. It includes a number of different ways that human beings come to be killed at the hands of other human beings. Before going on to read the rest of the chapter, read through the list and see if you would designate these causes of death as murder or as lawful killings. Reflect on why you think there are differences in the way these different means of killing might be dealt with differently in the law.

- Killing of an enemy solider during war

- State execution

- Killing a person who has threatened you with death or serious injury

- Stabbing an already dead body

- Doctor-assisted suicide

- Suicide

- Killing another person while driving when having consumed alcohol or illegal drugs

- A corporation failing to apply health and safety standards, and an employee is killed.

An avoidable death occurs when a human life ends when it could (and should) have been saved. Avoidable deaths include those that arise through the deliberately harmful actions of others (such as those defined as intentional homicide). But it also includes a large number of other forms of premature death, including, for example, those related to:

- deaths in the workplace

- self-inflicted deaths

- state killings

- people who die because of inadequate provision of shelter, warmth or food.

This considerably expands the categories of death outside of those that are normally focused on in criminal law. Indeed, critical thinkers on crime have asked 'what is to be lost (or gained) by focusing only on those avoidable deaths that are classified as "intentional homicide"?'

3.2   Social harm and social murder

People hold placards during a silent march for the launch of Justice for Grenfell. Criminologists have argued that because of acts of neglect or 'omissions' in policy, law and building procedures, the Grenfell fire can be understood as a form of social murder

An alternative way of defining the premature ending of a life, which has been adopted by criminologists, is 'social murder'. The philosopher Friedrich Engels (1845), in his book *The Condition of the Working Class in England,* gives a clear indication of how avoidable deaths can be caused systematically from the way a given society is set up and organised. In this book, Engels argues that structural inequalities (the inequalities between different social groups in society) mean some categories of people have lower or higher status in comparison to other categories of people and, as a result, those in the lower categories in a given society are the worst off.

> ...they inevitably meet a too early and an unnatural death, one which is quite as much a death by violence as that by the sword or bullet; when it deprives thousands of the necessaries of life, places them under conditions in which they cannot live – forces them, through the strong arm of the law, to remain in such conditions until that death ensues which is the inevitable consequence – knows that these thousands of victims must perish, and yet permits these conditions to remain, its deed is murder just as surely as the deed of the single individual.
>
> (p. 126)

While such avoidable deaths can be seen as more one of 'omission than of commission' (that is, neglect rather than intention), it is the social conditions that a person is living in that nevertheless 'undermines the vital [life] force gradually, little by little, and so hurries them to the grave before their time' (pp. 126–7). Death occurring sooner than it should for some people as a result of their living or working conditions is what is meant by 'social murder'. Compared to intentional homicide, social murder provides a way of considering a fuller range of avoidable deaths from which people may be at risk. To understand this wider view, we need to reconsider notions of 'harm' and 'responsibility' in the light of social murder.

Summary

- There are different ways of thinking about avoidable deaths, these include intentional homicide and social murder.

- The understanding of intentional homicide is linked to criminal law and includes an implicit requirement for 'criminal blame'.

4   Criminal blame and social responsibility

Section 3 critically questioned how an avoidable death must meet the criteria of 'criminal harm' before it can be defined as an intentional homicide. It was made clear that within the parameters of the law, a death must also meet the criteria of 'criminal blame' to be defined as intentional homicide. By contrast, examining avoidable deaths as a harm opens up an opportunity for a deeper understanding of what has happened. It helps us recognise who or what was responsible, and who, if anyone, should be blamed.

What are the strengths and limitations of the notion of 'criminal blame' when it comes to acknowledging and preventing avoidable deaths in the future?

The concept of blame is an important one within criminal law. In legal terms, and in some jurisdictions, the test of criminal liability or blame is expressed by the Latin phrase: *actus reus non facit reum nisi mens sit rea*. This literally means 'the act is not culpable or "at fault" unless the mind is guilty'. Therefore, for an event or action to be defined a 'crime', it must meet the requirements of 'intention', 'guilty mind' (or *mens rea*) and 'guilty action' (or *actus rea*). These terminologies, however, can differ according to jurisdictions.

When it comes to distinguishing the crime of intentional homicide from other unlawful homicides, the relevance of intention or blameworthiness may or may not be considered in legal proceedings: it all depends on the circumstances of the case and on the legal system of the country or state where the crime occurred. In addition, the question of whether or not there is an individual who can be blamed and found to be guilty is often asked. In short, when someone is killed people want answers!

Ideas about choice and the ways that social scientists and criminologists (in particular) consider different questions, claims and evidence in order to propose alternative ways of thinking about problems of crime and justice will be returned to throughout this book.

Reflective activity: To blame or not to blame …

Looking for who is to blame might seem to be an obvious response after a crime has taken place. But is the action of blaming really the only choice? Legal and philosophical scholars Nicola Lacey and Hanna Pickard (2015) have argued that in the United States and in the UK, the allocation of blame and calls for vengeance are common and are part of what is often referred to as a 'justice' model, associated with retribution. (Retribution is the idea that there should be some consequence or punishment inflicted on a person when they have committed an act that is wrong or criminal.)

That people should call for some kind of retaliation when harm has been done might seem like a 'natural' reaction, a universal response. However, Lacey and Pickard suggest that forgiveness is also a universal human adaptation. They suggest that human beings are naturally endowed with the capacity to blame or, alternatively, to forgive and repair. Choosing to blame or to forgive are decisions that societies and systems of law can make on the basis of social and cultural values. So, according to these authors, which option – blame or forgiveness – leads to the best outcome for society? Lacey and Pickard argue that blame is actually counter-productive and increases the risk of reoffending. They suggest that much more emphasis needs to be placed on the eventual outcome of a criminal process, which, in essence, requires envisioning a way for the 'perpetrator' to provide redress for the harm caused, be forgiven, and then welcomed back into society with the potential for a new future.

Think about the concepts of 'blame' and 'forgiveness' in relation to people in your own life that you feel have wronged you in some way. Are there merits or drawbacks to each of these responses to that wrong-doing? Reflect on what those might be and consider Lacey and Pickard's claims about blame being counter-productive.

As already mentioned, in many legal systems, an 'unlawful killing' is legally defined as murder when there is seen to be intentionality or what is legally known as *malice aforethought*. That is, for an intentional homicide to be deemed a 'murder', there must be a person or persons (the perpetrator(s)) with a state of mind that meets the legal requirements of 'malice'. This may include:

- the intention to kill

- the intention to cause bodily harm

- being recklessly indifferent.

These requirements for the application of criminal blame or 'culpability' in cases of murder may be viewed as somewhat limited as they cannot fully take account of all the complexities of human relationships or situations (Hulsman, 1991).

4.1 Criminal blame and corporate actors

The question of the usefulness of the notion of 'criminal blame' has been raised when it comes to the harms perpetrated by corporations and states. That is, the idea of 'criminal blame' is more often closely associated with the intentions and actions of individuals and their 'state of mind'. The idea of 'criminal blame' therefore is not very easily applied to the intentionality of corporate actors or to the 'minds of states'.

Consider, for example, the idea of health and safety crimes – that is, when people are injured or killed as a result of unsafe practices in the workplace. When prosecuting harms such as these, committed by corporations, it is very difficult to prove exactly 'who' the guilty party is and what their 'state of mind' was at the time of the death (Tombs and Whyte, 2009). The problem of workplace deaths is just one example that illustrates how criminal law is designed to hold individuals to account, not multinational corporations or states.

However, the Hazards Campaign (2017) estimate that, in the UK, 1200 workers die each year in work-related incidents (suicides, accidents on the road, in the air and at sea). Moreover, approximately 50,000 people die of illnesses, such as cancer or heart and lung diseases brought on by working practices, every year. In short, according to Hazards Campaign, about 140 people die every day due to the harmful consequences that arose while they were at work. These are generally deaths of people situated towards the lower end of the social ladder.

Health and safety crimes

Health and safety crimes include deaths that arise as a consequence of the actions and policies of corporations. Poor working practices can arise through breaches of health and safety regulations, long working hours, poor pay or insecure employment contracts.

The official Health and Safety Executive (HSE, 2017a) reported that 137 workers were killed in 'fatal accidents' at work in the Great Britain in 2016/17. This included people who died in the workplace because they were:

- run over

- hit by a moving object

- crushed by an object

- caught in machinery

- electrocuted

- fell from a height.

Attempts to expand the remit of criminal law to include the actions of corporations are under way in some countries. A significant example in the UK is *The Corporate Manslaughter and Corporate Homicide Act*, which came into force on 26 July, 2007. The offence that it brought into law is called 'corporate manslaughter' in England, Wales and Northern Ireland and 'corporate homicide' in Scotland (HSE, 2017b). Under previous law, a corporation could only be convicted of manslaughter if an individual company officer could be proven guilty of manslaughter and be identified as the 'controlling mind' of the company. In practice, it proved very difficult to prove that an individual was both the 'controlling mind' of the company and had the mental state to meet the requirements of a manslaughter charge. By contrast, the 2007 act stipulates that:

an organisation is guilty of the offence if the way in which its activities are managed or organised causes a death and amounts to a gross breach of a relevant duty of care to the deceased. A substantial part of the breach must have been in the way activities were managed by senior management

(UK Government, 2007, p. 3)

Criminal law historically has not been very effective when it comes to social murder or acts of gross negligence by corporations. Indeed, since the passing of *The Corporate Manslaughter and Corporate Homicide Act* (2007), very few prosecutions have resulted. In 2017, at the time of writing, only 25 prosecutions had been made.

So, who is responsible for the deadly harms that lead to social murder? When thinking about social murder, it is the deliberate and intentional policies of governments that have allowed the potentially deadly harms of social and economic inequalities to grow unchecked (Hancock and Mooney, 2013). Government laws and policies, both in terms of action and inaction that lead to inequalities, are political choices. This means that it is essential that criminologists understand avoidable deaths in the different social contexts in which they occur. Criminal law tends to focus only on those avoidable deaths that it narrowly defines within its framework as intentional homicide, while a great many harms in society are left outside of its remit. Moreover, when the factors that are connected to higher levels of avoidable deaths (including intentional homicide) are considered, it is shown that social and economic inequalities play a very large role. This leads to the question of how societies should handle the problem of social murder.

Talking about social murder is not just about looking at individual blame and intention. If the problem of avoidable deaths is framed through the language of social murder, then it makes sense that solutions should look to reverse the harms of inequalities. It means potentially taking a different approach to the way the harms in society are examined, thought about, and understood. This requires an alternative conception of responsibility for harm that goes beyond individual responsibility and the search for an individual murderer. This also, potentially, means thinking about a collective 'social responsibility' for reducing social harms as a whole (Scott, 2018).

Summary

- The law focuses on individual culpability.

- Criminal blame is not well suited to solving problems or addressing harm.

- Criminal law is not very effective in dealing with avoidable deaths / social murder.

- 'Social responsibility' is a future-orientated, social-policy-based answer to the 'murder puzzle', which aims to eliminate the social harms of structural inequalities and hold the powerful to account.

Conclusion

This chapter has highlighted different ways of thinking about the harm, blame and responsibility associated with avoidable deaths. You have considered the differences between those looking at avoidable deaths through the criteria of criminal law and those drawing upon the concept of 'social murder'. Criminal law has two key elements: criminal blame and criminal harm. This chapter questioned whether criminal harm is the best way to understand avoidable human deaths in profoundly unequal societies. This leaves us with a 'murder puzzle' – how should criminologists talk about and look to solve the problem of avoidable deaths? The chapter asked you to question whether criminal law is the best way to frame avoidable deaths.

The chapter then identified a number of problems with the application of criminal blame to all avoidable homicides and promoted in its place the idea of 'social responsibility'. Social responsibility is not backward looking, as the attribution of guilt or fault is, but rather it looks forward. Developing a 'non-blame' approach to addressing and responding to social problems requires us to look for the root cause of the problem, which can then hopefully be corrected. Taking responsibility, though, is not just restricted to suspected and supposed perpetrators of legally defined harms. Being socially responsible in relation to structural injustices means working together to transform structural processes in order to make social outcomes and human life chances more equal.

Throughout the chapter, and taking particular inspiration from the work of Dorling, you were invited to think about what is the most appropriate solution to avoidable deaths and if criminologists should be looking to promote social policies that can stop the biggest 'serial killer' known to us today: social and economic inequality.

References

Bambra, C. (2016) *Health Divides: Where you live can kill you,* Bristol, Policy Press.

Bárcena Ibarra, A. and Byanyima, W. (2016) *Latin America is the World's Most Unequal Region. Here's How to Fix it,* World Economic Forum [Online]. Available at www.weforum.org/agenda/2016/01/inequality-is-getting-worse-in-latin-america-here-s-how-to-fix-it/ (Accessed 29 November 2017).

BBC News (2017) *Homicide and knife crime rates 'up in England and Wales',* 27 April [Online]. Available at www.bbc.co.uk/news/uk-39729601 (Accessed 29 November 2017).

Department for Transport (2017) *Transport Statistics, Great Britain November 2017,* London, AMES Statistics [Online]. Available at www.gov.uk/government/uploads/system/uploads/attachment_data/file/661933/tsgb-2017-report-summaries.pdf (Accessed 30 January 2018).

Dorling, D. (2005) 'The usual suspects', in Hillyard, P., Pantazis, C., Tombs, S. and Gordon, D. (eds) *Beyond Criminology,* London, Pluto Press, pp. 178–91.

Engels, F. (1845) *The Condition of the Working Class in England,* Oxford, Oxford University Press (this edition 2009).

Equality Trust (2016) *How has Inequality Changed?* [Online]. Available at www.equalitytrust.org.uk/how-has-inequality-changed (Accessed 30 November 2017).

Hancock, L. and Mooney, G. (2013) '"Welfare ghettos" and the "broken society": territorial stigmatisation in the contemporary UK', *Housing, Theory and Society,* vol. 30, no. 1, pp. 46–64.

Hazards Campaign (2017) *Work Related Deaths: The Whole Story - Work-related injuries, illness and deaths,* Manchester, Hazard Campaign [Online]. Available at www.gmhazards.org.uk/wordpress/wp-content/uploads/2017/03/Hazards-Campaign-challenging-the-HSE-statistics.pdf (Accessed 30 January 2018).

Health and Safety Executive (HSE) (2017a) *Fatal Injuries Arising from Accidents at Work in Great Britain 2017,* London, HSE [Online]. Available at www.hse.gov.uk/statistics/pdf/fatalinjuries.pdf (Accessed 30 January 2018).

Health and Safety Executive (HSE) (2017b) *Corporate Manslaughter FAQs,* London, HSE [Online]. Available at www.hse.gov.uk/corpmanslaughter/faqs.htm (Accessed 30 November 2017).

Hulsman, L. (1991) 'The abolitionist case: alternative crime policies', *Israel Law Review,* vol. 25, nos. 3–4, pp. 681–709.

Lacey, N. and Pickard, H. (2015) 'To blame or to forgive? Reconciling punishment and forgiveness in criminal justice', *Oxford Journal of Legal Studies,* vol. 35, no. 4, pp. 665–96.

Malby, S. (2010) 'Homicide', in Harrendorf, S., Heiskanen, M. and Malby, S. (eds) *International Statistics on Crime and Justice*, Vienna, European Institute for Crime Prevention and Control, United Nations Office on Drugs and Crime (UNODC) [Online]. Available at www.unodc.org/documents/data-and-analysis/Crime-statistics/International_Statistics_on_Crime_and_Justice.pdf (Accessed 1 February 2018).

Marmot, M. (2004) *Status Syndrome,* London, Bloomsbury.

Marmot, M. (2015) *The Health Gap*, London, Bloomsbury.

Moms Demand Action (2013) 'Kinder Egg', *Moms Demand Action for Gun Sense in America* [Blog]. Available at https://momsdemandaction.org/kinder-egg/ (Accessed 23 April 2018).

NHS Scotland (2017) *Measuring Health Inequalities* [Online]. Available at www.healthscotland.scot/health-inequalities/measuring-health-inequalities/data-on-health-inequalities (Accessed 30 November 2017).

Office of National Statistics (2017) *Compendium: Homicide* [Online]. Available at www.ons.gov.uk/peoplepopulationandcommunity/crimeandjustice/compendium/focusonviolentcrimeandsexualoffences/yearendingmarch2016/homicide#what-does-the-long-term-trend-in-homicide-look-like (Accessed 30 November 2017).

Picketty, T. (2014) *Capital in the Twenty-First Century*, Cambridge, MA, Belknap Press.

Samaritans (2017) *Suicide Statistics Report 2017*, Surrey, Samaritans [Online]. Available at https://www.samaritans.org/sites/default/files/kcfinder/files/Suicide_statistics_report_2017_Final.pdf (Accessed 1 February 2018).

Scottish Government (2017) *Homicide in Scotland 2016-17. A National Statistics Publication for Scotland*, National Statistics, Edinburgh [Online]. Available at http://www.gov.scot/Resource/0052/00525786.pdf (Accessed 30 November 2017).

Scott, D. (2018) *Against Imprisonment,* Winchester, Waterside Press.

Skott, S. (2015) 'Homicide in Scotland: the need for a deeper understanding', *Scottish Justice Matters,* vol. 3, no. 3, pp. 36–7.

Statistica (2017) *Number of police recorded homicide offences in England and Wales from 2002/03 to 2016/17* [Online]. Available at www.statista.com/statistics/283093/homicide-in-england-and-wales-uk-y-on-y/ (Accessed 29 November 2017).

Taylor, I., Walton, P. and Young, J. (1973) *The New Criminology*, London, RKP.

Tombs, S. and Whyte, D. (2009) *Safety Crimes,* London, Routledge.

UK Government (2007) *The Corporate Manslaughter and Homicide Act 2007*, London, HMSO.

United Nations Office on Drugs and Crime (UNODC) (2013) *Global Study on Homicide*, New York, UNODC [Online]. Available at www.unodc.org/documents/gsh/pdfs/2014_GLOBAL_HOMICIDE_BOOK_web.pdf (Accessed 1 February 2018).

Wilkinson, R. and Pickett, K. (2010) *The spirit level: why equality is better for everyone,* Harmondsworth, Penguin.

Wilson, M. and Daly, M. (1997) 'Life expectancy, economic inequality, homicide, and reproductive timing in Chicago neighbourhoods', *British Medical Journal*, vol. 314, no. 7089, pp. 1271–4.

Young, J. (2010) *The Criminological Imagination*, Cambridge, Polity Press.

Chapter 6

Victims and perpetrators

by Deborah H. Drake and David Scott

Contents

Murder is defined in law as intentional homicide / death

avoidable deaths more often are unintentional from vantage of the individual premeditated killing.

So it is very difficult to situate instances of avoidable deaths as criminal murders.

On top of this, Social inequalities of wealth status and power, tend to influence our ideas about who perpetrators are and who victims are

Many powerful social groups benefit from their social status to both influence how they are perceived (as victim or perpetrator) and they have the power to evade criminal intent through criminal Justice system.

We see the twin influences of
i) narrow definition of criminal murder
b) social status/power
at work on cases of death in custody.

Introduction

Are all human lives equally important, or are some lives more important than others? The previous chapter highlighted great differences in wealth and status between different groups in societies all around the world, connecting economic and social inequalities with premature death. This chapter follows on from this discussion by considering how and when a person's death is labelled as a 'criminal act'. It is very often the case that whether a person's premature death is viewed as a crime depends on their power, status and respectability in society. In particular, this chapter focuses on the way the person who died is viewed by society, and whether their status or reputation has an impact upon levels of public sympathy for them and their family.

When somebody is killed, it may be expected that there will always be an attempt to provide an honest account of how the person died; that the memory and reputation of the deceased will be treated with dignity and respect; and that great efforts will be made to hold the perpetrator (or perpetrators) accountable. Yet this often depends on who the victim is, who the perpetrator is, and the circumstances surrounding their death.

In this chapter, you will be asked to think about whether certain victims attract more public sympathy than others and if certain perpetrators are presented as more villainous than others. Some victims may be considered less worthy of sympathy, in effect denying their victim status (Sykes and Matza, 1957; Cohen, 2001). Ideas about denying the extent of harm someone has suffered, or even denying that their death is a cause for grief and concern will be discussed in more detail in Chapter 7, but this chapter examines the potential denial of status as a victim when a person has died in state custody. The question of whether or not a person who has died at the hands of the state can or should be viewed as a victim has implications for the definition of crime.

Criminal law has been said to reinforce the status quo, or as in the title of philosopher Jeffrey Reiman's bestselling 1979 book, *The Rich get Richer and the Poor get Prison*. In this chapter, you will reflect upon the idea that the overall focus of criminal justice systems are on maintaining the existing order of things. This maintains and reinforces social and economic inequalities (as discussed in Chapter 7). This is because law-enforcement agencies are more often in contact with people who are from economically poorer backgrounds. The way both victims and offenders are defined must therefore take into account wider social, economic and political conditions.

In this chapter you will:

- explore how victims and perpetrators are defined
- consider ideas about the 'ideal victim' and the 'ideal enemy'
- explore the role of power and the state in the way unlawful and lawful killing is understood.

1   Defining the criminal or perpetrator

To understand the implications of crime and the way certain acts come to be made illegal, or are 'criminalised', it is important to understand how the meanings of acts and events are socially constructed. ('Social construction' can be defined as the process by which ideas have been created and accepted by people in a given society (adapted from Merriam-Webster Dictionary, 2011)). One example of a social construct is the idea that people fall into different social classes. Labelling some people as 'working class' or 'upper class' and what is thought and said about them as a consequence are all dependent on common social values, meanings and beliefs. The application of labels have real consequences for the lives of those labelled.

Although acknowledging ideas or concepts that are social constructs will come up repeatedly throughout this book, it is helpful to recognise at this point that seeing an idea as a social construction is a way of taking a step back and asking, for example, 'Who says this is a social problem – and what sort of social problem do they think it is?' (Clarke, 2001, p. 266). Focusing on how ideas are socially constructed is important because they shape criminal justice policies and practices.

Reflection activity: How a society defines what is legally deemed to be a crime

Try taking a step back and asking the following questions:

- Who defines what a crime is?

- If stopping crime is about minimising harm to people, then why do preventable harms occur in society that do not come under the criminal justice system?

- Whose interests are best served by existing constructions of crime?

When it comes to defining an act as a crime, what has happened is generally regarded as harmful. Yet there is no clear objective criteria connecting the wide range of actions brought together under the label 'crime'. Crime is not only a social construction: it is also an historical construction. That is, its definition changes depending on when an event occurs and where an event occurs (Christie, 1986a). But it also depends upon the identity of both the victim and the perpetrator.

1.1   The criminal law and the state

The state performs a key role in defining and enforcing (or, as will be discussed later in this chapter, *not* defining and enforcing) the criminal law. Historically, the use of the criminal law has been one of the main strategies in the control and regulation of those who are often poorest and most disadvantaged in terms of social, educational and employment opportunities (Hall et al., 1978). Criminologists have long identified how prisons have been used to control homeless people and unemployed people, especially in times of economic downturn (Rusche and Kirchheimer, 1939; Reiman, 1979).

Prisons are places where societies tend to send their poor, unemployed and under-educated

Criminalisation and the processes by which people are held to account through a criminal justice system also perform a key role in enhancing state power. The control and regulation of certain populations that are considered to be 'troublesome' – people who are seen as on the outside of society, such as alcoholics, benefit recipients, protestors, sex workers, irregular migrants – makes the state look strong. This has led to a number of criminologists pointing to the wider role of crime control as a political tool to both stir and then soothe social anxieties (Cohen, 1973; Hall et al., 1978).

One of the means by which politicians can do this is by publicly condemning or even creating laws that target people 'on the margins' of society. This is sometimes referred to as **'scapegoating'**.

Scapegoating is not only applied to criminalised situations, it can also be used in other, more general, situations. The idea that certain activities or people may be brought under public scrutiny more often or more easily than others, does not deny that crimes – as officially defined and applied – have taken place, nor that those identified by law enforcement have not perpetrated such offences. What is important here is the recognition that crime is sometimes used as a political tool. This means that governments can draw public attention towards particular behaviours, and explanations for social problems as crimes, which may be equally usefully thought about or explained in other ways.

How a crime is defined is often linked to the social and economic backgrounds and differing levels of power held by the people involved. Whether somebody is young or old, black or white, rich or poor (and, of course, all categories in between) influences both how and when people or actions might be viewed as 'criminal'. As the time and place of an activity or event also influences whether an activity is defined as a crime, it should perhaps come as no surprise that many criminologists contest the concept of crime.

While the law and its enforcement can, and does, protect people and while many crimes that are recorded in the official figures are focused on vulnerable and/or impoverished individuals, the agencies of criminal law perform a key role in maintaining structural divisions in society. Sociologist Mary Baumgartner (1992) makes an important contribution to the debate on the relationship between law enforcement and social and economic inequalities. She argues that the application of the rule of law is closely tied to specific stereotypes about *who* is the criminal.

Scapegoating
Scapegoating refers to the process of blaming an innocent person or group of people.

1.2   Stereotyping the criminal

A stereotype is 'a widely held, but fixed and oversimplified image or idea of a particular type of person or thing' (Oxford English Dictionary). Stereotypes are not always inaccurate, but they are often too simplistic to account for the diverse range of people or issues that they are trying to describe. Stereotypes are often drawn along lines of race, gender, sexuality, culture or other defining groups. For example, a gender stereotype is that men are physically strong. A cultural stereotype might be the idea that French or Italian people are the best lovers.

Stereotyping 'the criminal'

A headline in the Glasgow-based *Evening Times* online, posted on the 19 November 2017, read: 'Yob Who Attempted to Intimidate Young Man Asked: 'Do You Want to Fight a Ned?'

The *Evening Times* article describes a confrontation on a train platform that led to an individual being charged with acting in an aggressive manner. The event did not include any physical contact between the perpetrator and the people who complained about the incident. However, the headline identifies the aggressor in the story as a 'Yob'. 'Yob' is a slang term used in the UK to identify a person who, generally speaking, is young, male, aggressive and/or rude. The word derives from the word 'boy' spelled backwards and is a derogatory term. Interestingly, in this story, the aggressor also refers to himself as a 'ned'. A 'ned' is a slang term often used in Scotland to refer to a young hooligan or petty criminal. Both terms are stereotypes and are used to construct the idea that these groups of people are troublesome and to be condemned and feared. The person in question in this story has, evidently, absorbed the stereotype or label that he perceives society has bestowed upon him and, indeed, the newspaper reconfirms the construction of the young person in this way by referring to him as a 'yob'.

(*Evening Times*, 2017)

The image of an aggressive looking man with a knife (left) is much more in keeping with ideas of 'the criminal', yet Dr Harold Shipman (right), who does not fit this stereotypical image, was one of the most prolific serial killers in history

There is a constant flow of images, stories, headlines and debate on crime in the media, but these representations of both crime and 'the criminal' are often crudely constructed to focus on highly visible 'street crimes' that generally are perpetrated by young men and women from socially and economically disadvantaged backgrounds. Those who are criminalised are also disproportionately from Black, Asian and Minority Ethnic (BAME) communities. Many other harmful activities, such as those perpetrated in the home, the workplace or through the actions or inactions of state agencies, are either relatively invisible or are not popularly (or sometimes legally) considered as crime (Tombs and Whyte, 2003). The prioritisation of certain harms as illegal, and the extent to which laws which target them are enforced, provide only a partial picture of the problem of crime. Baumgartner (1992) argues that in the history of law enforcement, the offenders who have been criminalised largely have three factors in common.

1 **Social distance**: they have been successfully placed at considerable social distance – this means that, before they are criminalised, they have already been successfully defined in society as different, as people who are 'not like us', or are 'outsiders'.

2 **Respectability**: a negative reputation has been established about the offender – they are seen as an 'enemy' or their status is lower

in contrast to the victim of their offence, who was considered highly respectable and had or has higher social status.

3   **Social position**: they are poor, disadvantaged or from a 'low' social class and therefore do not have access to legal advice and representation.

For Baumgartner (1992), *social distance, respectability* and *social position* inform the assessments of the moral character of the offender and provide the context for the reproduction of stereotypes that make it more likely for there to be unfair outcomes. Not only are some voices more likely to carry influence than others, but people are treated differently by law-enforcement agencies because of their social and economic backgrounds.

Summary

- Crime is a social construction. The application of the 'criminal' label reflects social divisions and stereotypes.

- Law enforcement has historically been related to social position, respectability and the social distance between victim and offender.

2 Defining the victim

The previous section calls to attention the question of who has the 'power to define'. In many societies around the world, there are social hierarchies. People at the top of the social hierarchy (sometimes also referred to as the social ladder) might be, for example, politicians, celebrities or very rich people. At the lowest end of the social hierarchy (at the bottom of the ladder), might be people who are homeless or jobless or even just those who are working in low-paid, insecure jobs. The exact positions or classifications within a social hierarchy will differ between different societies and at different points in time. This is important because those in the most powerful positions in a given society can give greater authority and credibility to particular viewpoints or ways of understanding the social world. This is sometimes referred to as 'privileging' certain sources of knowledge.

One way to imagine this is to consider the idea of a society where all decisions are based on religious law – that is, on ideas espoused in the Bible or the Quran or another religious text. In this society, then, religious knowledge would be 'privileged' over other forms of knowledge – such as scientific evidence, for example. From this example, it is evident that 'knowledge' is not always objective, impartial or even evidence-based. Moreover, it can be very difficult to challenge forms of knowledge that have come to be 'privileged' in a given society because, very often, those who hold the most power in that society will use this knowledge to maintain the existing order of things.

It is essential to recognise the importance of power and the existence of social hierarchies when thinking about problems of crime and justice, because power plays a central role in the way the problem of crime is defined. The way in which power shapes the creation of knowledge has been described as a 'regime of truth' (Foucault, 1980, p. 133). What this means is that those who hold the power in society often have the authority and credibility to influence what is deemed as worthy of attention, and *who* is to be believed or disbelieved. Within a 'criminal' context, the authority, power and influence of a person – both victim and perpetrator – is linked to their social status and position on the social ladder (Foucault, 1991). In social hierarchies, not all voices are heard, and not all speakers are viewed with the same standing, or subsequently offered a fully equal opportunity to offer their version of an event or to argue their position.

In situations where a crime or harm against someone has occurred, it is not only the social standing of the perpetrator that might fall under scrutiny: social hierarchies play a role in the way victims are defined too. There is no certainty that when someone experiences emotional, psychological, physical or financial harm, it will be *recognised* as a form of harm. The acknowledgment of someone as a victim can lead to sympathy for that person's plight. However, the denial of this victim status (or 'victimhood') is also possible, leading to an absence of compassion, care and empathy for those who have been harmed.

The word 'victim', for many people, immediately brings to mind the idea of 'victims of crime'. However, there are many other circumstances to which the word 'victim' might apply. For example, there are victims of torture, war, natural disaster, famine or disease. Linking the word 'victim' to the issue of crime at all is a relatively new development. In the post-war period (roughly late 1940s to 1970s), the term 'victim' in Britain was more often used to describe people who were 'victims of misfortune', such as poverty, disease, lack of education and lack of access to clean water or sanitation (Mawby and Gill, 1987). In this sense, they were victims of social injustice.

The idea of 'the victim' of crime began to gain attention with the work of prison reformer, Margery Fry, in the 1950s. She argued that the state response to crime should not only focus on the 'offender' or perpetrator, but that victims should be compensated and that some restitution or 'payback' should be afforded to them (Fry, 1951). The 1960s and 1970s can be seen as the start of a 'victims' movement' in criminal justice, particularly in the United States, but also in the UK. This movement (now better described as victims' *movements*, as more than one exists) gained momentum through campaigning and activists working to raise greater social awareness of domestic violence, sexual assault and rape, and child abuse, including incest.

The victims' movements of the 1970s included those protesting violence against women, such as this rally in City Hall Plaza, Boston, United States, on 26 August 1976

Over time, 'victims of crime' began to gain more and more attention in the media, in criminal justice policy-making and in public awareness. Recognising the victim and their needs can be seen as a step forward in creating more balanced, fair and honest responses to crime and social disharmony. However, there is often a mismatch between the way victims are imagined, who they really are and what they actually want to happen in response to what they have been through.

2.1   The ideal victim

The Norwegian sociologist Nils Christie (1986a, 1986b) considered the way that victims of crime and those who commit crimes are often represented in the media, in government policy and even, sometimes, in the minds of the general public. He suggested that victims are often thought and talked about in very general terms, and as if most victims of crime are 'ideal victims'. An 'ideal victim' is 'a person or category of individuals, who – when hit by crime – most readily are given the complete and legitimate status of being a victim' (Christie, 1986b, p. 18). The 'ideal victim', then, is someone who deserves the most public sympathy and compassion and is seen as entirely blameless, innocent and absolutely undeserving of whatever has happened to them. Christie (1986b) sets out six attributes that he argues contribute to the image of the 'ideal victim'.

1   The victim is weak, particularly in relation to the offender – here the victim could be sick, elderly, a child, a vulnerable woman or a combination of these.

2   The victim is respectable and not perceived to have been doing anything 'wrong'.

3   The victim is innocent of any wrong-doing him or herself.

4   The victim does not know the perpetrator of the crime.

5   The 'offender' is unquestionably a 'bad' person.

6   The victim is powerful enough to be heard but not so forceful that he or she could challenge existing power structures and vested interests currently protected in the law.

According to Christie, 'ideal victims do not necessarily have much to do with the prevalence of *real victims*' (1986b, p. 27, emphasis in original). The ideal victim is a good and deserving individual who is completely innocent of the harm that has happened to them. They are non-threatening and easy to empathise with. But this version of the idea of victim can also be viewed as a stereotype. Stereotypes are important in presenting to us both the 'ideal victim' and the 'ideal enemy'. What becomes very important when it comes to defining an act as criminal is the interface between the offender (who perpetrated the act) and the ideal victim (who is the victim).

While Christie's image of the 'ideal victim' is not pure fiction – there are real individuals who meet all of his criteria – the problem with the image of a 'perfect' victim is that often there are victims of crime who do not meet these expectations. Think, for example, about someone in prison who is brutally beaten by another person in prison. This victim will, generally speaking, not be viewed with the same sympathy as somebody who is brutally beaten in front of their house.

Christie also goes on to describe the counterpart to the 'ideal victim', the 'ideal enemy'. The 'ideal enemy' or the 'typical' (sometimes called 'archetypal') offender is a person who is dangerous, underserving, 'big and bad'. The less 'human' a perpetrator appears, the more human the victim (Christie, 1986a, 1986b). In other words, the victim is more deserving of sympathy and acknowledgement when the perpetrator is seen to be especially wicked.

But, just like the 'ideal victim', there is a problem with the image of the 'ideal enemy' when they turn out to be simply unfortunate, desperate or foolish as opposed to wicked. Think, for example, of a parent who steals food for their children or someone who gets into a seemingly minor fight and, after one punch, their victim falls backwards, hits their head on the concrete and dies. These are situations where the stereotype of the 'ideal enemy' or 'archetypal offender' does not quite match up with reality. Moreover, when a person comes to be labelled as 'an enemy' in society, it can be difficult for them to be viewed by the public, media or by official authorities as worthy of rights or other protections. To explore this issue, the next section considers the problem of deaths in custody.

Summary

- Since the 1970s, there has been increasing emphasis on the views and opinions of victims of crime.

- The 'ideal victim' (Christie, 1986b) is the person most likely to receive sympathy and support for the harm they have experienced.

3   Deaths in custody

The loss of a life at the hands of another human being is a shocking event that requires a social response, but it is important to note that not all deaths that occur in this way are viewed or officially handled with the same level of sympathy. The strict legal definition of intentional homicide (or murder), as discussed in Chapter 5, means that there are only certain circumstances when the killing of a human being at the hands of another is viewed as a crime.

Despite the obvious limitations of the idea of an 'ideal victim' or an 'ideal enemy', these stereotypical images can often spring to mind when considering the most serious of crimes, such as intentional homicide. Sometimes, in media accounts, a homicide victim might be, in essence, blamed for their own death. For example, if a drug addict is killed by another person in the course of obtaining drugs, the victim in this case may be blamed for getting into this situation in the first place.

The social constructions of those deemed to be 'good' and those deemed to be 'bad' mean that it is not always easy to see those who have been labelled as 'bad' (such as the drug addict in the example above) as victims, even when they have been seriously harmed. There are very clear messages conveyed in the media, for example, when it comes to defining who is deserving of public sympathy and who is not. Often, those who are convicted of a crime and sent to prison are perceived as undeserving of public sympathy. They are 'the enemy', to be disliked, defeated, condemned and ostracised. The police and other workers in law enforcement are presented as people who are here to protect law-abiding citizens and to uphold the rule of law. They are here to 'do good' and ensure the safety and wellbeing of the public. But when people die at the hands of the state or state agents, the question of who is 'good' and who is 'bad' becomes more difficult to answer, as the following newspaper article shows.

Three Prison Officers Charged with Assaulting Inmate at Forest Bank

by Neal Keeling

Three officers at Forest Bank prison in Salford have been charged with assaulting an inmate.

The charges relate to an alleged incident in the reception area of the jail. The alleged incident took place on December 14, 2016.

In a separate case an officer and a manager at Forest Bank have been charged with theft and money laundering.

That case follows a police investigation into reports of the theft of computer games, DVDs, and CDs from the prison.

Two prison officers were sacked in 2015 at Forest Bank for posting cruel remarks on Facebook after a young prisoner died in custody.

The pair made inappropriate comments about the death of Ashley Gill, 25, who died in jail in Liverpool after suffering an asthma attack.

Another prison officer at Forest Bank was demoted over the same issue and several others disciplined.

(Keeling, 2017)

So, it seems important to ask: can a criminal be a victim? Can a victim be a criminal? Can someone who is responsible for upholding the law be either a victim or a criminal? There are not necessarily easily drawn boundaries between victims and criminals. They may sometimes be the same people, but perhaps at different times in their life course. It cannot be assumed that even though someone is employed to uphold the law that they will do so in all circumstances. It may, though, be harder to label and view someone as a 'criminal' when they do not fit the criminal stereotype, such as when police or prison officers break the law. When someone dies at the hands of law-enforcement agencies, this is referred to as 'a death in custody'.

Death in custody

The term 'custody' refers to the position of being detained in a prison, a police station, special hospital, psychiatric unit or any other institution where an individual is in the care or supervision of criminal justice practitioners. A 'death in custody' refers to the sometimes controversial circumstances surrounding the death of a suspected or convicted offender while under the care and supervision of law-enforcement agents. However, 'a death in custody' can also occur after the person has been released if they suffered injuries while in custody that subsequently lead to that person's death.

As police officers are people with considerable authority and relatively high social status, their voices are more likely to be believed than someone who has little social status or is considered as dishonest because of their previous lawbreaking. These differences in status between law enforcers and the people who are most likely to be criminalised (and therefore most likely to die in state custody) are important as this is likely to influence both the levels of public sympathy and also whose story is going to be believed.

3.1   Victim blaming

'Victim blaming' occurs when the victim is perceived as living a 'high risk' lifestyle, such as someone who uses drugs, has previously been convicted of a criminal offence, or is otherwise viewed as not living as carefully as they should have. People who die in police or prison custody are often viewed as 'at fault' for their own deaths. This is especially so if it can be established that they are drug users, alcoholics, abusers, serious/career criminals or 'social misfits', who are viewed as failures. Victims who die in these circumstances are often not discussed in the media or other public arenas with much sympathy, nor are the perpetrators of their deaths discussed with much hostility. The actions of the powerful perpetrator are negated and excused, and the powerless victim silenced, while existing stereotypes are reinforced. A victim's negative reputation (Scraton and Chadwick, 1987) distracts attention from the status and guiltiness of the perpetrator, while also being a way of minimising the 'criminal harm' of the victim's death.

"Relax - we'll blame it on Curiosity."

If curiosity killed the cat, is the cat effectively 'victim blamed' for their own death?

Reflection activity: Victimhood

Acknowledgement of victimhood is shaped by various factors, not just the extent of harm a person experiences but also who they are and who has harmed them. This is a particularly important consideration when someone dies in state custody. Here the interconnections between state, power, and crime can be observed.

- How likely is an event to be defined as a crime if the state is involved in the harm caused?

- Will the criminal law be used to hold the agents of the state to account?

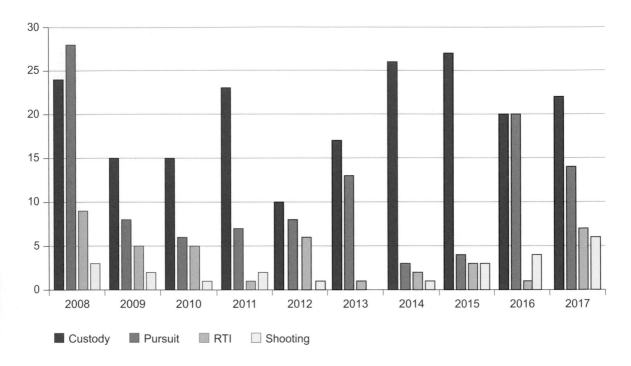

Figure 6.1 Deaths in police custody, England and Wales 2008–2017

The graph in Figure 6.1 (INQUEST, 2017) summarises data on deaths in custody from England and Wales between 2008 and 2017.

The independent charity INQUEST recorded over 5,600 deaths in prison and police custody in England and Wales alone between 1990 and 2016. Between 2002 and 2012, there were over 380 fatalities in England and Wales as a result of police shootings or following contact with the police, and 290 deaths in police vehicle incidents (INQUEST, 2017). Deaths in state custody make up a high number of the avoidable deaths recorded each year. But, in fact, the scale or detail of such deaths are rarely covered in the media. To explore the details of the way such deaths can occur, the death of Christopher Alder provides a useful, illustrative example.

Summary

- Deaths in state custody highlight problems around the divide between 'ideal victims' and 'ideal enemies'.

- People who die in state custody have sometimes been blamed for their own deaths, thus distracting attention away from state responsibility and accountability.

4 The death of Christopher Alder

Christopher Alder (1960–1998)

On 1 April 1998, Christopher Alder, a 37-year-old former paratrooper, died on the floor of Queen's Garden Police Station, Hull. He had been a victim of an assault outside the Waterfront nightclub. He had been hit in the mouth and knocked to the floor, and was subsequently taken to Hull Royal Infirmary to address his cut lip and missing tooth. Following an argument with medical staff – Christopher Alder had been discharged from the hospital but still felt he required further treatment – he was escorted from the hospital, arrested for breaching the peace, handcuffed and put in the back of a police van. Although he walked into the back of the van, he was carried out. He was dragged into the station and left motionless face down on the floor of the custody suite with his trousers around his knees for 11 minutes. Thirteen minutes after his arrival, the police noticed he had breathing problems and then called an ambulance. Despite attempts at resuscitation, Christopher Alder died on the police station floor.

At the post-mortem, it was revealed that he had additional head injuries to those recorded at the hospital before his arrest. There was also mud on his knees, indicating that he may have been taken out of the police van during transit to the police station. Although five police officers were suspended from duty, his death was never treated as a possible intentional homicide: neither the police van that transported him, nor the custody suite where he was held, were ever investigated as crime scenes. Items of Christopher Alder's clothing (such as his belt) were lost. The clothes of the police officers involved were tested but the results were never revealed and the officers' clothes were later destroyed. An **inquest** was held to investigate the death. At the inquest, the suspended police officers exercised their rights to refuse to answer a number of key questions about their actions preceding the death. The jury unanimously found that Christopher Alder had been unlawfully killed.

Inquest
An inquest is a judicial inquiry that examines the facts relating to a particular incident, usually death.

Although the Crown Prosecution Service (CPS) initially brought a charge of gross negligence manslaughter against the officers, at their trial the judge directed the jury that the only 'safe' verdict they could reach was one of not guilty. This happened directly after the case by the prosecution, so the defence was never asked to give any evidence and none of the police officers were ever asked any questions in a legal court about Christopher Alder's death.

4.1 *Rough Justice*

Following the collapse of the trial, the BBC television series *Rough Justice* commissioned a programme into the death. Broadcast on 14 April 2004, 'Death on Camera' included CCTV footage of the last 11 minutes of Christopher Alder's life. Following the broadcast of the programme, there were widespread calls for a public inquiry into his death. The Independent Police Complaints Commission (IPCC), which operates in England and Wales, published their report into his death on 27 March 2006 (IPCC, 2006). While the IPCC report criticised four of the five officers involved for the 'most serious neglect of duty' and recognised that racism was a factor in his death, it refused to endorse calls for a public inquiry.

The family of Christopher Alder, especially his sister Janet Alder, campaigned tirelessly for truth and accountability in the days, weeks, months and years following his death.

Janet Alder

In November 2011, the government formally apologised to the Alder family in the European Court of Human Rights. It was admitted that there had been failures in how Christopher Alder had been dealt with by the police that amounted to 'inhuman and degrading' treatment. It was also admitted that there had been failures around the preservation of the right to life, and that the state had not undertaken an effective and independent inquiry following his death.

However, in the same month it was also revealed to the Alder family that his body was still in Hull Royal Infirmary, more than 13 years after he died. Rather than Christopher, the Alder family had buried a 77-year-old woman called Grace Kamara in 2000.

In July 2013, the IPCC revealed that it had received evidence from the police that Janet Alder had been subjected to intensive police surveillance and espionage. Fourteen different police officers had been deployed to spy on her. Much of this surveillance, including bugging of meetings with legal representatives, had not been 'properly authorised' (and hence was illegal). The CPS initially decided not to prosecute the officers in charge of her surveillance because there was insufficient evidence, but in November 2017 they determined that there had been enough evidence to bring gross misconduct charges against two Humberside Police detective sergeants.

It is evident from Christopher Alder's case that he was not viewed as an 'ideal victim'. (Remember that the reason he had gone to hospital was because he had been the *victim* of an assault.) The fact that he did not receive the treatment he felt he needed was the reason he was angry and disruptive at the hospital, where he was subsequently arrested. From that point onwards, he was treated as a 'criminal', not a victim. It might be imagined that if Christopher Alder more closely fitted Nils Christie's (1986b) idea of the 'ideal victim', he would never have been arrested in the first place, nor died in custody. He was not considered by the police to be a vulnerable person who required protection, but rather as a potentially dangerous man who was misbehaving.

Summary

- The death of Christopher Alder in police custody has been hugely controversial.

- The family of Christopher Alder, most notably Janet Alder, has struggled for 20 years to hold the state responsible for his death.

- Christopher Alder is a tragic example of someone who did not meet the criteria of the 'ideal victim' (Christie, 1986b).

5   Conclusion

This chapter has shown that who is 'the criminal' and who is 'the victim' is not always obvious, and that many factors influence how both 'the criminal' and 'the victim' are viewed. Those who hold the most power in society play a role in how crime, criminals and victims are defined. Moreover, those who hold the least power in society can more easily fall victim to negative stereotypes, injustices and, in the most extreme and tragic cases, death at the hands of the state. The role of power in defining crime and enforcing the criminal law leaves ordinary members of society less able to act against the harms that the powerful cause (Tombs and Whyte, 2003).

Criminal law is only rarely used (and barely ever successful) in prosecuting law-enforcement agents who are implicated in the death of someone in their custody. Victims of death in custody are overwhelmingly from lower social and economic backgrounds and are unlikely to fit neatly into the 'ideal victim' classification. By downplaying the victimhood of those who have died in custody, for example, wider issues concerning the way governments use and exercise their power are neglected (Scraton and Chadwick, 1987).

References

Baumgartner, M. P. (1992) 'The myth of discretion', in Hawkins, K. (ed.) *The Uses Of Discretion*, Oxford, Oxford University Press, pp. 129–62.

Christie, N. (1986a) 'Suitable enemies', in Bianchi, H. and van Swaaningen, R. (eds) *Abolitionism: Towards a Non-Repressive Approach to Crime*, Amsterdam, Free University Press, pp. 42–54.

Christie, N. (1986b) 'The ideal victim', in Fattah, E. (ed.) *From Crime Policy to Victim Policy*, New York, St Martin's Press, pp. 17–30.

Clarke, J. (2001) 'Social constructionism', in Muncie, J. and McLaughlin, E. (eds) *Sage Dictionary of Criminology*, London, Sage, pp. 266–8.

Cohen, S. (1973) *Folk Devils and Moral Panics*, London, Routledge.

Cohen, S. (2001) *States of Denial*, Cambridge, Polity Press.

Evening Times (2017) 'Yob who attempted to intimidate young man asked: "Do you want to fight a ned?"', *Evening Times*, 19 November [Online]. Available at www.eveningtimes.co.uk/news/15668588. Yob_who_attempted_to_intimidate_young_man_asked___Do_you_want_to_-fight_a_ned__/ (Accessed 17 May 2018).

Foucault, M. (1980) 'Two lectures', in Gordon, C. (ed.) *Power/Knowledge: Selected Writings of Michel Foucault*, London, Longman, pp. 78–108.

Foucault, M. (1991) 'Questions of method', in Burchell, G., Gordon, C. and Miller, P. (eds) *The Foucault Effect*, Chicago, University of Chicago Press, pp. 73–86.

Fry, M. (1951) *Arms of the Law*, London, published for the Howard League for Penal Reform by Gollancz.

Hall, S., Critcher, C., Jefferson, T., Clark, J. and Roberts, B. (1978) *Policing the Crisis*, London, Macmillan.

Independent Police Complaints Commission (IPCC) (2006) 'Report, dated 27th February 2006, of the Review in to the events leading up to and following the death of Christopher Alder, 1st April 1998', London, Stationery Office [Online]. Available at http://news.bbc.co.uk/1/shared/bsp/hi/pdfs/27_03_06_alder.pdf (Accessed 18 May 2018).

INQUEST (2017) *Unlawful killing conclusions and prosecutions* [Online]. Available at https://www.inquest.org.uk/unlawful-killing-conclusions-and-prosecutions (Accessed 5 May 2018).

Keeling, N. (2017) 'Three prison officers charged with assaulting inmate at Forest Bank', *Manchester Evening News*, 15 September [Online]. Available at https://www.manchestereveningnews.co.uk/news/greater-manchester-news/prison-officers-assault-forest-bank-13626041 (Accessed 22 May 2018)

Mawby, R. and Gill, M. (1987) *Crime Victims: Needs, Services and the Voluntary Sector*, London, Tavistock Publications.

Miriam-Webster Dictionary (2011) s.v. 'Social Construction'

Oxford English Dictionary (n.d.) s.v. 'Stereotype'

Reiman, J. (1979) *The Rich get Richer and the Poor get Prison*, London, Wiley.

Rusche, G. and Kirchheimer, O. (1939) *Punishment and Social Structure*, London, Transaction Press (this edition 2006).

Scraton, P. and Chadwick, K. (1987) 'Speaking ill of the dead', in Scraton, P. (ed.) *Law, Order and the Authoritarian State*, Milton Keynes, Open University Press.

Sykes, G. and Matza, D. (1957) 'Techniques of neutralisation: a theory of delinquency', *American Sociological Review*, vol. 22, pp. 664–70.

Tombs, S. and Whyte, D. (2003) *Unmasking the Crimes of the Powerful*, London, Peter Lang Publishing Inc.

Chapter 7

Dangerous states

by Deborah H. Drake and David Scott

Contents

STATE IS EMPOWERED TO PRESCRIBE

WHICH OF THE FOLLOWING

premature, unlawful, ~~unwanted~~, Avoidable

unavoidable Deaths

are classified avoidable unlawful

can subsequently achieve the

criminal status of murder/intentional

criminal Status of murder/intentional

homicide.

↙

Criminal Justice System   attribute blame to
provides the institutional   individuals
apparatus to restrain   at individual) (and
this process to   at individual)
perpetuate

Capacity to transform   Murder = Prove intent to
social harm/murder into   Murder = Prove Blame

Introduction

What is the role of 'the state' in society? Is it to rule, regulate and control? Is it to protect, mediate or facilitate human well-being? Is it to do all of these things or none of them? And what protections and systems of regulation are there in place to regulate or control the role of the state itself? How can citizens know if a given state is operating in the best interests of society? What can be done when states act violently towards their own citizens?

This chapter is concerned with exploring the problems of 'state crime', and when states seem not to act in the best interests of citizens. In some states, harms perpetrated by the state can be difficult to detect, are easily explained away or are hidden; while in others, state crime is more blatant and overt. Harms of the state can include (but are not limited to):

- bombing or otherwise waging war against their own people

- declaring illegal wars against other states

- manipulating a state's laws to benefit certain segments of a population while disadvantaging others.

One example of state-perpetrated harm that can easily remain hidden involves illegally extending benefits and tax breaks to multinational corporations. In 2017, after a three-year investigation, the European Commission (which is the politically independent executive arm of the European Union) found that Ireland had extended illegal tax benefits to Apple and that the multinational company owed €13 billion in back taxes. As part of the same investigation, it was found that Luxembourg had extended illegal tax benefits to Amazon and that the company owed €250 million in back taxes. Margrethe Vestager, the European Commissioner for Competition, stated that 'Amazon was allowed to pay four times less tax than other local companies subject to the same tax rules. Member states cannot give selective tax benefits to multinational groups that are not available to others' (*Financial Times*, 2017).

These examples demonstrate that those in power often have opportunities to commit illegal acts without the consent or the knowledge of the wider population whom they are intended to serve. Privilege and position offer opportunities to which many people in society do not have access. These opportunities provide ways and means of obscuring their actions or of deflecting attention away from the activities of the powerful (Cohen, 2001; Coleman et al., 2009). The previous two chapters explored how intentional homicides and other avoidable deaths have been defined (or not) as crimes by the state. The centrality of the state in the process of establishing the rules and laws of society raises some fascinating questions when state officials – or the state itself – kills or when it is in breach of those very rules and laws. If the state defines the actions and behaviours that are deemed illegal in society through enacting laws, who has the power to check up on the activities of the state itself?

In this chapter you will:

- explore the question 'What is state crime?'
- consider state violence as a form of state crime
- investigate questionable state practices and avoidable deaths through a case study of Syria
- consider the difficulties associated with holding states to account, including the role of human rights discourses.

1   What is state crime?

The idea of 'state crime' might, at first, appear to be a problem that happens elsewhere, as something that could not or would not happen in your state (Green and Ward, 2004). However, almost any state is potentially capable of committing acts that are illegal.

Reflective activity: Thinking about crimes of the state

Have you ever thought about the actions of the state as potentially being unlawful or harmful? Can you think of any examples of harms perpetrated by states, either historically or more recently? As you read through this chapter, think about the various ways that states may act in ways that might be illegal, or even violent, and consider how difficult it is to challenge such actions.

Thousands of shoes collected by the Nazis from the victims of genocide at Auschwitz, Poland, during the 1940s

As one of the most extreme and commonly referenced examples, consider the actions of the German, Nazi government in both the lead up to and during the Second World War.

Between 1933 and 1945 more than 11 million men, women and children were killed by the Nazi government in the Holocaust; around six million of whom were Jews (Bauman, 1989; Levy, 2001). This is one of the most extreme examples of state crime and violence that has ever happened. The mechanisms by which the Holocaust was accomplished – the means by which it was seemingly, legally, carried out, and the powerlessness (or reluctance) of people to stand against it – offer enduring lessons about the potential powers of the state and the need for vigilance of state authority. Rummel (1994) estimates that from 1900 to 1987 over 169 million people were killed by states. You might be surprised to learn that this very high number actually *excludes* a further estimated 35 million deaths that occurred in wars (including 'avoidable deaths', such as those of the Holocaust, which are considered war crimes).

Any state can make decisions that affect its whole population by, for example, setting out social policies, implementing particular strategies for ensuring social order, or deciding to go to war with another state. It is this understanding of 'the state' – as a unified body of actors, acting together (and with authority) according to a given political agenda – that is often the basis for a starting point for understanding that 'state crime' tends not to be perpetrated by a single individual, but by a group of people acting together.

Four categories of state crime

Criminologist Eugene McLaughlin breaks down the notion of 'state crime' into four possible categories:

- **Acts of political criminality**, including: censorship, corruption, intimidation, manipulation of the electoral process.

- **Criminality associated with the security and police forces**, including: war-making, genocide, ethnic cleansing, torture, disappearance, terrorism, assassination.

- **Economic crimes**, including: monopolisation practices, violations of health and safety regulations, illegal collaboration with multinational corporations.

> - **Social and cultural crimes,** including: deliberate economic impoverishment of sections of society, institutional racism and cultural vandalism.
>
> (Adapted from McLaughlin, 2012, pp. 289–90)

In addition to McLaughlin's definitions, the harms perpetrated by states have also been defined by some criminologists as fundamental breaches of human rights (Schwendinger and Schwendinger, 1975; Cohen, 1993; Stanley, 2006). Mass atrocities, genocides and state-sanctioned killings are often understood as a breach of the 'right to life'. The Equality and Human Rights Commission (EHRC), which has sub-commissions responsible for Scotland and Wales, stated that:

> Human rights are basic rights and freedoms that belong to every person in the world from birth until death. They apply regardless of where you are from, what you believe or how you choose to live your life ... These basic rights are based on values like dignity, fairness, equality, respect and independence.
>
> (Equality and Human Rights Commission, 2017)

The language of human rights has been used by the families of victims killed by state actions or actors as a way of calling attention to the state as a potential perpetrator of violence and harm. The extent to which such rights can be effectively legislated for and protected when the power of a state is turned against its own people is a problem that some criminologists have highlighted (see Schwendinger and Schwendinger, 1975; Green and Ward, 2004) and will be discussed in the next section.

1.1 How to think about state crime and violence

One of the difficulties associated with thinking about the harm and violence perpetrated by a state is being able to recognise when and where it is happening. The state holds significant powers in society, including:

- control over policing and security firms, the military, and systems of surveillance

- the authority to enact and overturn laws

- the ability to create regulations and policies

- the power to influence how these policies are discussed in society.

(Watts, 2016)

The powerfulness of state agents prompts such questions as: who polices the police? Who monitors the appropriateness of state systems of surveillance? In short, who can intervene and control an 'out of control' state?

Devastation in Aleppo as a result of the Syrian civil war

There is considerable difficulty associated with challenging harms perpetrated by the state and, as a result, state crime is one of the most serious forms of social harm.

There are four reasons why this is the case:

1 The state can officially and lawfully exercise violence. As a result, the powers of the state can be used to inflict human rights violations against its own people and foreign nationals living within its borders.

2 The state is the primary source of laws and this provides it with the ability to define what is against the law and, crucially, what is not.

3 The state's control of the institutions and personnel of the criminal justice system allows it to target and subdue anything or anyone that threatens it – either economically, socially or politically.

4 The state is in the strategic position to conceal its criminality.

(Adapted from McLaughlin, 2012, pp. 289–90)

For criminologists Julia Schwendinger and Herman Schwendinger (1975), the problem is that states ultimately have the power to create laws. As you have read, a crime in a given state is only defined as such by the laws in place at a given time. As such, states have the ability to avoid defining their own actions as crime or even changing the law to ensure that their actions are not strictly illegal. Schwendinger and Schwendinger (1975) have argued that the legal definition of 'crime' is therefore problematic when considering harms perpetrated by the state. They thought the evaluation of what is harmful in society could not be determined by legal definitions alone. As an alternative, they suggested that the suffering of human beings ought to be the measure by which state actions are evaluated, not the state-defined criminal law.

Despite the ambitions of the Schwendingers' thinking, there are several problems with their idea. First, while it aims to broaden the way criminologists think about crime, it lacks precision in the definition of what constitutes a violation of human rights. Criminologist Stanley Cohen (1993) provided a counter-argument suggesting that, by the Schwendingers' logic, the economic exploitation of people could be viewed as equivalent to genocide. Cohen argued that: 'By any known criteria, genocide is more self-evidently criminal than economic exploitation. The Schwendingers make no such distinction nor try to establish the criminality of human rights violations' (Cohen, 1993, p. 98).

For Cohen, the Schwendingers fail to address either the problem of human-rights violations by states, or how to prevent them happening in the first place. Furthermore, if human-rights violations are not legislated for through state institutions – such as the criminal, administrative or civil law – by what power can the state be held to account? Finally, even if human rights violations were somehow legislated for under criminal law, this would not address some of the problems discussed in Chapter 5 about criminal blame. Using human rights as the basis to identify a state crime would lead only to the punishment of individuals (if appropriate individual responsibility could be established). They could not recognise collective social responsibility, which is how states operate. Nor could human rights address the inequalities in power that result in corruption and create the possibility for genocide and other state killings in the first place. However, these counter-arguments do not mean that human rights are irrelevant or cannot be used to leverage change, rather it should be recognised that there are no easy or straightforward ways to hold states to account.

Summary

- Because the state holds the power to define the law, they also have the power to avoid it.

- Recognition of the importance of human rights may provide some basis by which to evaluate the actions of states, but the extent to which human rights can be legislated for and protected remains unresolved.

2   Deviance, social control and the state

In order to evaluate more carefully the way states operate and how they can avoid scrutiny and challenges, it is useful to consider the sociological concepts of 'deviance' and 'social control'. At the level of the individual, deviance can be defined as: any violation of rules or 'norms' (social expectations that influence or guide behaviour). For example, in some societies, it might be viewed as deviant for a person to have facial tattoos, but in others it may be a form of cultural or religious expression. What is viewed as 'deviant' differs between different societies and even between different groups within a society (Dellwing, Kotarba and Pino, 2014).

5   *definition of deviance*

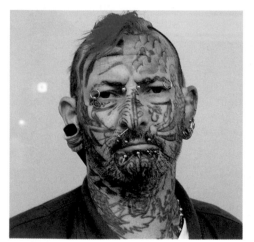

A 'deviant' tattooed man (left), traditional tattoos on face of a Maori warrior (right)

When a person acts in a way that others view as inappropriate or deviant, this action can be censored, ridiculed or otherwise condemned either formally or informally by other people (as discussed previously in Chapter 1). This is where 'social control' can come in. This refers to both the formal and informal means of enforcing norms in a society or among a group (Cohen, 1985). Social control can be applied by family members, among friendship groups, by employers in workplaces, by powerful groups in whole societies, or by governing states.

Importantly, it is not just at the individual level that the idea of deviance and the problem of how to exert social control can apply.

deviant
states

Professors of Law, Penny Green and Tony Ward, have argued that 'states or state agencies engage in deviant behaviour as well as practices that violate legal norms' (2004, p. 2). The state itself may act in ways that are not acceptable to its own citizens or to the international community. States, therefore, can be seen as 'deviant' – that is, not acting in ways that either their citizens or other nations think is appropriate or which are illegal. Deviant states, however, have the power to try and control the extent to which they are viewed as deviant by justifying their actions or attempting to hide their illegal activities. This prompts the question: who holds the power to deem a state as deviant or dangerous? Is there any way social control could be exercised over unruly states?

George Orwell's *Nineteen Eighty-Four*

In 1949, English novelist George Orwell published *Nineteen Eighty-Four*. This book describes a fictional version of the world, divided into three super-states: Oceania, Eurasia and Eastasia. The story that the book describes is set in the super-state of Oceania. Here, Orwell's main character, Winston Smith, struggles with state oppression. Oceania is a place where individuality and free thinking are discouraged by the Party (the state) and a variety of methods are utilised to watch and scrutinise every human action. The citizens of Oceania are subjected to surveillance by the 'thought police', or 'Thinkpol'. Thinkpol aim to discover and punish thought crime, defined as personal and political thoughts that are not approved by the state. In Oceania, personal relationships are discouraged and, as a result, citizens do not trust each other. Even small children are used by the Party to inform on their parents or other adults who may not be conforming to the regime.

In *Nineteen Eighty-Four*, fear is utilised as a means of controlling and manipulating citizens to follow the political regime as set out by the prevailing political party. People have no control over their own lives and live in misery, under repressive social and political conditions. The idea of a place, like Oceania, where people lead dehumanised and fearful lives provides an extreme example of what life could be like in an oppressive state.

Although the ideas in *Nineteen Eighty-Four* and the super-state of Oceania were fictional, at different points in history oppressive regimes, such as Orwell describes, have been a reality for some societies.

Some political systems are more vulnerable to deviant state practices than others because they have fewer ways for citizens to contribute to political decisions and fewer checks and balances to hold the state to account. For example, in the case of authoritarian forms of state, such as dictatorships, the individual freedoms of people are subordinate to the state: the state is not responsible to the people. In this kind of state, the idea of citizens holding any powers that challenge the state is effectively designed out of the whole system. What do such regimes, then, look like from the perspective of citizens? Can such systems be challenged by citizens or by other states?

Summary

- Deviance and social control are key concepts that can be considered in relation to the state as well as to individuals.

- Some states can more easily engage in deviant practices because their political systems have fewer checks and balances on the way they utilise their power.

- It can be difficult to exercise any form of control over a 'deviant state'.

7
Syrian
example.

8
UK / Saudi
example

3   Syria: a deviant state?

Syria is a state in the Middle East. It shares its longest border with Turkey to the north and is also bordered by Iraq on the east, Lebanon and the Mediterranean Sea to the west and Israel and Jordan to the south. Two of its largest cities, Damascus and Aleppo, are among the oldest inhabited cities in the world (McHugo, 2015).

Syria and its border states

The population of Syria is ethnically and religiously diverse. The largest ethnic groups are Syrian Arabs and Bedouin Arabs. Kurds form the largest minority, but Syria also has small numbers of Turks, Assyrians, Circassians and Armenians (Smith et al., 2017; Sousa, 2017a). The most common religious groups are different Islamic groups – including Sunni, Alawites and Druze – and Christians (Smith et al., 2017; Sousa, 2017b). Historically, Syria was vulnerable to invasion from nearly every direction and has previously been ruled and occupied by powers from elsewhere (McHugo, 2015). Between 1923 and 1946 Syria was ruled by France, the French having gained control over the area that included Syria in the early 1920s. France was then assigned Syria as part of the League of Nations' mandate, which had resulted from the Paris Peace Conference that ended the First World War. This mandate stipulated that the governing state (in this case, France) could act as trustee until the citizens of a particular region could effectively manage themselves and become an independent state.

In 1946, Syria gained independence from the former French mandate and became a parliamentary republic. Syria was politically and socially unsettled in the period immediately following its independence. Instability and struggles for power continued until the government was overthrown during the coup in 1963, when the Ba'ath Party assumed power.

Syria's political system is officially intended to be a unitary republic, which means that no regions or cities have autonomy or are self-governed (Smith et al., 2017). As a republic, it should function similarly to a democracy: both tend to use a representational system whereby citizens vote to elect politicians to represent their interests. Indeed, a republic is often viewed as a type of representational democracy with checks and balances, intended to safeguard the rights of the people (including minorities) set out in a constitution. According to its officially declared political system, Syria is intended to be governed by an elected president who is accountable to its citizens. However, the ruling political parties have long practised a highly authoritarian regime with most of the political power in the hands of the al-Assad family. This was possible because, between 1963 and 2011, it was ruled under 'Emergency Law', which suspended most of the rights and protections of citizens (McHugo, 2015). Thus, since 1963, it has resembled a dictatorship more than a republic. Emergency law was lifted in 2011 and a new constitution was brought in to force in 2012.

In order to understand the ramifications of the authoritarian, repressive and deviant regime that operated in Syria in the latter decades of the twentieth century and in the first decade of the twenty-first century, it is helpful to work backwards from the outbreak of the revolution or civil war that began there in 2011.

3.1 The Arab Spring and the Syrian revolution

On 17 December 2010, Mohamed Bouazizi, a 26-year-old Tunisian street vendor, doused himself with gasoline in a busy street, outside the Tunisian governor's office and lit himself on fire. He subsequently died of his injuries in hospital on 4 January, 2011. What would make someone go to such extreme lengths as a form of protest? Bouazizi committed this desperate act out of frustration with a relentlessly repressive regime in Tunisia. It was subsequently reported that Bouazizi had been targeted by police for years. He was a poor street vendor, trying to make a living selling vegetables. However, he did not have the money to buy a permit or to bribe police officials to continue his street vending. On the day of his act of protest, he had been publicly humiliated by a municipal official who confiscated his scales and overturned his vegetable cart.

Demonstrators in Tunisia hold a portrait of Mohamed Bouazizi (1984–2011) during a demonstration in Tunis, Tunisia, on 28 January 2011

Bouazizi's story is significant because his extreme act of protest is considered to have begun what was to become known as the 'Arab Spring'. Following his act of protest, and between December 2010 and March 2011, several protests broke out in other North African and Middle Eastern states, including (among others) Algeria, Jordan, Egypt, Sudan and, finally, Syria. Just as in Tunisia, the unrest in Syria began with an incident that sparked off anger in large segments of the population. In March 2011, 15 children between the ages of nine and 15 years graffitied the walls of their school in the southern town of Daraa. The graffiti called for the fall of the regime. Security officials arrested the children and took them to Damascus where they were detained and tortured.

As McHugo (2015, section IV) notes, the children:

> … may have been copying events of other Arab countries which they had seen on television, or perhaps they were repeating the discontent which they had heard their parents voice in the privacy of their families … In any event, they were school children, not adults.

Peaceful protests erupted first in Daraa, calling not for a regime change, but for reform (Phillips, 2016). However, security forces and authorities responded to the demonstrations with extreme force, killing several people in Daraa. As a result, the protests spread to other cities and some segments of the population began to call for President Bashar al-Assad to step down. However, the regime responded to the outbreak of the protests across Syria with violence and brutality. A summary of the conflict by international relations scholar, Christopher Phillips, reads:

> The Syrian civil war is the greatest human disaster of the twenty-first century. Since conflict broke out in 2011, over 470,000 have been estimated killed and 1.9 million wounded. Over 4.8 million have fled the country and 6.6 million more are internally displaced, more than half the pre-war population of 21 million. A United Nations report estimated that by the end of 2013, Syria had already regressed 40 years in its human development. Two years later half of its public hospitals had been closed, barely half of its children were attending school and over 80% of Syrians were living in poverty … Thousands of cases of long-absent diseases such as typhoid and measles returned due to a lack of vaccination. Large parts of Syria's cities were rubble. The

economy was in ruins. Hundreds of the country's precious cultural heritage locations, including five of its six UNESCO world heritage sites, had been damaged or destroyed. The average life expectancy of a Syrian dropped from 70 to 55 in four years.

(Phillips, 2016, p. 1)

Previous chapters have highlighted the nature and extent of avoidable deaths and problems around defining deadly harms as crimes. The situation in Syria further highlights this complex relationship between premature deaths, crime, harm and the state.

3.2   The al-Assad regimes – the dangers of authoritarian states

How did Syria and the other Middle Eastern and North African states end up involved in such deadly conflicts with their own people? In Syria, political power has been concentrated among a small and select group, led by the al-Assad dynasty.

Hafez al-Assad came to power as resident of Syria in 1970. This was accomplished with the support of the armed forces in Syria (McHugo, 2015). As already stated, the state had been under Emergency Law since the coup of 1963. Officially, this was due to the ongoing conflict between Syria and Israel. However, Hafez al-Assad, operating under so-called 'emergency measures', legitimately implemented a repressive and authoritarian regime over the Syrian people. People could be arbitrarily arrested, tried, sentenced or otherwise detained on the grounds of 'protecting the state' (Phillips, 2016, p. 45). In effect, this included anyone who dared to speak out against Assad or challenged his rule. One of the main tools of the Assad regime was the *Mukhabarat* or intelligence services – made up of '50,000–70,000 security officers willing to utilise fear, torture and intimidation routinely' (Phillips, 2016, p. 45). Throughout the final decades of the twentieth century, Assad operated a regime in Syria that very much resembled the imagined world of *Nineteen Eighty-Four*. When Hafez al-Assad died in 2000, his son, Bashar al-Assad, succeeded him. Despite hopes for reform, the Syrian people were subsequently met with a continued authoritarian rule, which many began to rebel against with the arrest of the 'graffiti boys' in Daraa in March 2011.

It is important to recognise that the Syrian people would not have unanimously condemned the authoritarian rule of the Assad regime. However, the devastation and scale of harm and death that has been caused by the conflicts in Syria still warrant scrutiny – both by all factions of Syrian society and the international community.

Reflective activity: Challenging states

Can or should anything be done to intervene when a state is perpetrating violence, including torture and murder, against its own citizens?

State sovereignty – the right of a ruling government to manage its own domestic affairs in its own way – is difficult to question. Should an international body or external state power have the right to challenge the authority of another state body, even when it has seemingly been elected by a large proportion of the population? At the same time, is it acceptable to just stand by when there is evidence of continued serious conflict, torture and avoidable death being perpetrated by a state against even a minority of its own people?

Summary

- Syria can be seen as an example of a state governing in ways that are questionable and that has ultimately led to ongoing conflict, violence and death.

- Even when there are seemingly appropriate checks and balances in place to protect citizens from authoritarian rule, such protections can still be overruled and dismissed by the power of the state. This can leave potentially large segments of a population vulnerable to considerable fear, threat and danger from those in power.

4   How can states be called to account?

There are few formal 'social control' measures that can be exercised against a state. Moreover, there is often considerable difficulty in gaining widespread international agreement over when another state should attempt to intervene. One form of international social control of the 'deviant state' are human rights covenants and treaties. Human rights protections and conventions set out by the United Nations were intended to avoid the possibility of a repeat of the extreme atrocities and human rights violations that took place during the Second World War.

How human rights should help regulate states and protect citizens

The Universal Declaration of Human Rights (UDHR) is the foundation for many human rights frameworks and laws within individual states. It is viewed as the foremost statement of the rights and freedoms of all human beings and was adopted by the General Assembly of the United Nations in 1948. It sets out a range of rights and freedoms to which everyone, everywhere in the world, is supposed to be entitled. This includes, for example, the right to life and freedom from torture, inhuman or degrading treatment. This declaration, along with two covenants (which are promises by states to its citizens) makes up the International Bill of Human Rights. These two covenants are:

- the International Covenant on Civil and Political Rights (ICCPR, adopted 1966)

- the International Covenant on Economic, Social and Cultural Rights (ICESCR, adopted 1966).

These latter two documents are intended to provide the legal force behind the UDHR. The ICCPR is intended to commit the states that have signed up to it to protect and respect the civil and political rights of individuals.

(Adapted from Equality and Human Rights Commission, 2017)

Despite these agreements, human rights are extremely difficult to enforce. For example, human rights violations in Syria have long been under scrutiny and criticism from international organisations, such as Amnesty International, Human Rights Watch and others. Freedom of speech, freedom of association and assembly were strictly controlled in Syria for over forty years and yet there was no significant challenge to these violations by external bodies. Syria remains a signatory to the International Covenant on Civil and Political Rights but, up until the civil war began in 2011, it has remained virtually unchallenged. The difficulty is, in part, that there are no clear means by which to question, challenge or intervene when sovereign states act in deviant, harmful and deadly ways. To a certain extent, this is due to the power held by state bodies (as discussed in earlier sections of this chapter). However, it is also, potentially, due to problems of denial, discussed in the next section.

4.1   State of denial

In his landmark study, *States of Denial: Knowing about Atrocities and Suffering*, the central concern of Cohen (2001) is how ordinary people deny or acknowledge the suffering of others. (To be in 'a state of denial' is to block out or repress or to simply avoid acknowledgment of something, in this case human suffering.) Some psychologists and medical professionals might argue that being in denial may well be a viable coping mechanism and, in certain circumstances, can be the best thing to do, especially for a period of time (Kramer, 2010). However, when it comes to social problems, denial often means inaction and failure to intervene to help others. The opposite of denial is acknowledgement. Acknowledgement means recognising what is taking place and trying to intervene to make a difference. This can involve all sorts of different actions, but key among them is the act of questioning a situation wherein other human beings are suffering, being harmed or killed.

For Cohen (2001), there are three main ways people deny knowledge of suffering.

- Strategies of *literal denial* deny assertions of human rights infringements or that atrocities actually occurred. In this view, such atrocities are not acknowledged to have happened at all.

'State of denial'

'collective preservation'

(a)

- *Interpretive denial* is a way of giving an act or event less problematic interpretations. In this case, a harm is reinterpreted so that it appears as less serious. It is a way of closing down debate by claiming that, although something happened, it just wasn't very serious.

- *Implicatory denial* arises when people recognise the reality of human suffering but deny any personal responsibility.

Building on the insights of fellow criminologists Gresham Sykes and David Matza (1957), Cohen identified seven forms of implicatory denial, which he referred to as the 'techniques of denial'.

1 *Denial of responsibility*: A person denies they are fully or even partially responsible for human suffering they have directly witnessed or caused, but did nothing to stop. It was not their fault, it was an accident, or it was not intentional. The perpetrator, or observer, claims ignorance of what has occurred.

2 *Denial of injury*: What happened did not hurt. There was no or only limited damage caused. The action was harmless or the suffering created insignificant.

3 *Denial of victim*: There is no identifiable victim of the action. The sufferer has lost their claims to being a victim by precipitating the action themselves or undertaking an action that led to them being harmed: 'They brought it on themselves'.

4 *Condemnation of the condemners*: The person who is complaining should be condemned. They may be hypocrites, liars or not seen as a respectable person or an authority who can make such accusations.

5 *Appeal to higher loyalties*: That the harm was done for the greater good. The suffering serves wider purposes, personal commitments, ties, bonds and beliefs. Somebody else is a more deserving person to be labelled a victim.

6 *Denial of knowledge*: This is when people claim they have no knowledge of certain events. There are gradations of knowing, and there is a fine line between knowing and consciously not knowing.

7 *Moral indifference*: The suffering of the other is acceptable. There is nothing to be explained away. Moral indifference arises when

people become desensitised to suffering, emotionally overloaded, or when they distance themselves from others, seeing 'the other' as a lesser being.

According to Cohen, individuals and societies have a moral responsibility to help others in need. Human suffering must not be accepted irrespective of who the person is, where they are from, or what they have done. He also warns of the danger of 'intellectual denial', where the moral foundations of truth and justice are denied by academics. He argues that criminologists should explore human suffering in the many manifestations that have been denied, or where there is only limited political action aiming to address such suffering. For Cohen, it is never morally acceptable to deny the suffering of others and to remain silent when it is possible to speak and be heard. His analysis raises important questions about how states and their citizens should respond to learning about mass atrocities, such as the harms perpetrated by the Syrian state.

4.2   Why human rights matter

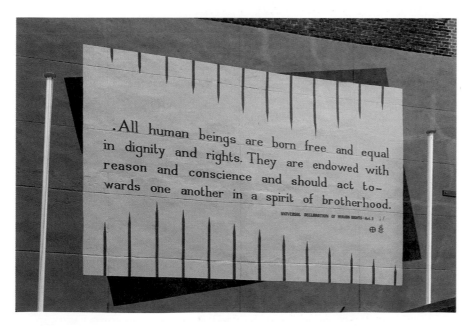

Mural from Article 1, Universal Declaration of Human Rights

Criminologist René van Swaaningen (1997, p. 234) provides a simple, yet powerful, basis for thinking about human rights. He argues that recognising human rights can be as simple as asking the question 'are

177

you suffering?' Human suffering arises when a person is denied something that is their inalienable right to have, such as the right to life, freedom from torture, and protection from inhuman or degrading treatment. Refusing to recognise such inalienable human rights is a means of effectively denying claims to the full experience of what it means to be human.

Like the Schwendingers' (1975) human rights arguments discussed earlier, this approach to human rights is also not without its critics. It has often been argued that inalienable or 'human' rights are simply principles that have been invented to serve certain interests (Douzinas, 2000). Critics have argued that definitions of human rights merely reflect the social, economic and cultural ideas dominant at the time they were invented. Attempts to identify the essential aspects of human life are steeped in controversy, and may provide only partial definitions of the human experience. What is worse, these partial accounts of human life (which emphasise the perspective of the white, male, middle class, Western world) may even be used as the basis justifying the very actions they are supposed to be preventing – that is, dehumanising practices against groups that are not included in this limited definition of humanity (Bauman, 1989).

These concerns about human rights are important, but an acknowledgement of the social, political and historical constructions of the *content* of human rights, does not automatically mean that the *concept* of human rights should be abandoned. Indeed, there can be no basis for critiquing *dehumanisation* if there is no acknowledgement that certain aspects of 'being human' must always be carefully protected and safeguarded everywhere. Importantly, the recognition that a shared humanity exists independently of social, legal, historical, and political constructions provides the baseline from which critical value-judgements of inhumanity can be made (Scott, 2016).

Human rights cannot be built on the innocence, vulnerability or perfection of those who are suffering. It is not just the 'ideal victims' (Christie, 1986) – whom you read about in Chapter 6 – who should be considered as deserving human rights. Nobody is less or more deserving or worthy of being recognised as a human being. Everyone, by the virtue of their humanity, deserves to have certain rights protected. This means, of course, being protected from other people but crucially it also means being protected from the harms of the state. As outlined above, the drafting of the Universal Declaration of Human Rights was in response to the horrors of the Holocaust and other mass murders of people by their own government or those of invading states. Human rights have been 'invented' as a protective shield against state power and the harms and crimes committed by states (Cohen, 1994). Yet, despite these intentions, there are significant weaknesses with current human rights protections and the international bodies meant to hold states to account on violations of these rights.

Can states ever be held to account? Human rights provide a language that can be more forcefully used to shield and protect the powerless and vulnerable, through guaranteeing procedural safeguards and minimum legal standards. They can also be utilised as a mechanism by which to evaluate and highlight the stark and dehumanising practices of a state (van Swaaningen, 1997; Cohen, 1998). But the language of human rights is not just about laws and legal sanctions. It may be easy to fall back upon 'techniques of denial' to generate inaction and complicity with harms perpetrated by states. However, human rights can, and are, used to shame states through evidence of dehumanisation highlighted in the media, campaign groups and the actions of ordinary people who wish to acknowledged the suffering and entirely avoidable deaths of others. The idea of human rights can be tied to forms of power, whether that be informally through the power of people, or more formally – through legal powers and mandates.

Summary

- The UDHR and its covenants are frameworks intended to help protect all human beings from inhuman and degrading treatment by arbitrary or authoritarian state powers.

- The denial of human suffering is a key issue to be overcome and some criminologists, like Stanley Cohen, argue that the acknowledgement of suffering is a social responsibility all human beings share.

- Although human rights frameworks are difficult to enforce, the language of human rights provides a baseline by which to evaluate the performance of states and acknowledge the suffering of others.

Conclusion

This chapter asked you to think about when states kill or commit otherwise harmful acts against their own people. This has highlighted the importance of clarifying the rights to which all human beings are entitled. The notion of human rights moves beyond definitions of crime that are predicated only on criminal law (Stanley, 2006). The focus on human rights (and especially the 'right to life') in criminology continues to gain momentum that may, over time, provide a means by which to better highlight when they are breached and violated. As an alternative to following a state-set agenda that merely reflects the interests of the powerful, it is important for criminology to ask difficult questions that highlight when dangerous states are acting against the interests of citizens and are not being held to account for those actions.

References

Bauman, Z. (1989) *Modernity and the Holocaust*, Cambridge, Polity Press.

Christie, N. (1986) 'The ideal victim', in Fattah, E. (ed.) *From Crime Policy to Victim Policy*, New York, St Martin's Press, pp. 17–30.

Cohen, S. (1985) *Visions of Social Control: Crime Punishment and Classification*, Cambridge, Polity Press.

Cohen, S. (1993) 'Human rights and crimes of the state: The culture of denial', *Australia and New Zealand Journal of Criminology*, vol. 26, no. 2, pp. 97–115.

Cohen, S. (1994) 'Social control and the politics of reconstruction', in Nelkin, D. (ed.) *The Future of Criminology*, London, Sage, pp. 63–88.

Cohen, S. (1998) 'Intellectual scepticism and political commitment: the case of radical criminology', in Walton, P. and Young, J. (eds) *The New Criminology Revisited*, London, Palgrave Macmillan, pp. 98–129.

Cohen, S. (2001) *States of Denial: Knowing about Atrocities and Suffering*, Cambridge, Polity Press.

Coleman, R., Sim, J., Tombs, S. and Whyte, D. (2009) *State, Power, Crime*, London, Sage.

Dellwing, M., Kotarba, J. and Pino, N. (2014) *The Death and Resurrection of Deviance: Current Ideas and Research*, London, Palgrave.

Douzinas, C. (2000) *The End of Human Rights*, London, Hart.

Equality and Human Rights Commission (2017) 'What are human rights?' [Online]. Available at www.equalityhumanrights.com/en/human-rights/what-are-human-rights (Accessed 22 May 2018).

Financial Times (2017) 'EU takes Ireland to court over Apple taxes', 4 October [Online]. Available at www.ft.com/content/fac76fd1-7cf6-3abb-8fad-5cebfd6d96bd (Accessed 1 February 2018).

Green, P. and Ward, T. (2004) *State Crime: Governments, Violence and Corruption*, London, Pluto Press.

Kramer, U. (2010) 'Coping and defence mechanisms: What's the difference? Second act', *Psychology and Psychotherapy: Theory, Research and Practice*, vol. 83, no. 2, pp. 207–21.

Levy, P. (2001) *The Holocaust: Causes*, Austin, Raintree Steck-Vaughn Publishers.

McHugo, J. (2015) *Syria: A Recent History* [ebook reader], London, Saqi Books.

McLaughlin, E. (2012) 'State crime', in McLaughlin, E. and Muncie, J. (eds) *Sage Dictionary of Criminology*, 3rd edn, London, Sage, pp. 289–90.

Orwell, G. (1949) *Nineteen Eighty-Four*, Harmondsworth, Penguin (this edition 2004).

Phillips, C. (2016) *The Battle for Syria: International Rivalry in the New Middle East*, London, Yale University Press.

Rummel, R. J. (1994) *Death by Government*, New York, Transaction Publishers.

Schwendinger, H. and Schwendinger, J. (1975) 'Criminology and human rights', in Taylor, I., Walton, P. and Young, J. (eds) *Critical Criminology*, London, Routledge and Kegan Pau, pp. 113–46.

Scott, D. (2016) 'States of denial', in Taylor, P., Corteen, K. and Morley, S. (eds) *Companion to State, Power and Civil Liberties*, Bristol, Policy Press, pp. 257–9.

Smith, C. G., Hamidé, A-R, Irvine, V. E., Gadd, C. J., Commins, D. D., Ochsenwald, W. L., Polk, W. R. and Scullard, H. H. (2017) 'Syria', *Encyclopaedia Britannica* [Online]. Available at www.britannica.com/place/Syria (Accessed 22 May 2018).

Sousa, G. (2017a) 'Largest Ethnic Groups in Syria', Worldatlas [Online]. Available at www.worldatlas.com/articles/largest-ethnic-groups-in-syria.html (Accessed 22 May 2018).

Sousa, G. (2017b) 'Religious Beliefs in Syria', Worldatlas [Online]. Available at www.worldatlas.com/articles/religious-beliefs-in-syria.html (Accessed 22 May 2018).

Stanley, L. (2006) 'Towards a criminology for human rights', in Barton, A., Corteen, K., Scott, D. and Whyte, D. (eds) *Expanding the Criminological Imagination*, London, Routledge, pp. 168–97.

Swaaningen, R. van (1997) *Critical Criminology*, London, Sage.

Sykes, G. and Matza, D. (1957) 'Techniques of neutralization: a theory of delinquency', *American Sociological Review*, vol. 22, pp. 664–70.

United Nations (1949) *Universal Declaration of Human Rights*, New York, UN.

Watts, R. (2016) *States of Violence and the Civilising Process: On Criminology and State Crime*, London, Palgrave Macmillan.

Chapter 8

The death penalty:
state-sanctioned murder?

by Deborah H. Drake and David Scott

Contents

Introduction

A criminal justice system is the means by which a society identifies, processes and responds to people who have broken or transgressed its criminal laws. In many societies, the fundamental purpose of the criminal justice system is to identify who is to blame for a particular act of wrongdoing and to proclaim and deliver an appropriate response, usually a form of punishment. In Chapters 5 and 6, you explored 'criminal blame' and 'criminal harm', and how they are central to the application of the criminal law. This chapter takes that discussion forward by critically examining ideas about punishment and, specifically, the death penalty – the most severe of all punishments. The death penalty is the legally sanctioned killing of an individual by the agents of a state. As you have read in the previous chapter, states have often killed their own citizens, but this is not always explicitly lawful. Chapter 7 also highlighted the importance of human rights as a means of critiquing and holding the state to account. For its critics, the death penalty is an expression of the violation of the most basic human right by the state: the denial of the right to life.

When it comes to the power of the state to kill its own citizens, moral arguments promoting the right to life may be neutralised by 'techniques of denial' (which you read about in Chapter 7), such as the 'denial of victim', where the person who died is not considered as someone meriting compassion or sympathy (Cohen, 2001). Is the death penalty 'state-sanctioned murder' or is it a justifiable action, intended to serve the greater good of society as a whole? This chapter explores the evidence for and against the death penalty, but also questions the reasons why societies punish, the goals that are thought to be achieved through the use of punishment, and the underlying moral and cultural values that shape ideas about punishment. Human rights are an important consideration in these discussions: they comprise the basic values that many societies around the world have tended to judge as essential for human wellbeing and are therefore worth protecting. And some of these values, as this chapter will discuss, are undermined by severe state punishments. In the case of the death penalty, this chapter asks you to question whether the deliberate taking of a life by the state is justifiable or if, conversely, it undermines the social values such an action is seeking to promote.

In this chapter you will:

- explore details of the nature and extent of the death penalty around the world, focusing on the death penalty in the United States where some areas still retain this punishment and where strong views are held both for and against its use

- critically examine the ethical and political justifications of the death penalty and how these are used to distinguish state executions from intentional homicide

- consider the arguments for and against the death penalty and focus on the importance of state power when thinking about the content and enforcement of the criminal law.

Content Note

Please be aware that this chapter contains images of methods of executions currently used in the United States, which you may find disturbing.

1   The death penalty today

Although the death penalty has existed at different times all across the world, by 2018 it was abolished in all of Europe (with the exception of Belarus). Many nations with a highly developed economy and advanced technology and industry have also banned the death penalty (the main exceptions are the United States, China, Japan, Singapore and Taiwan).

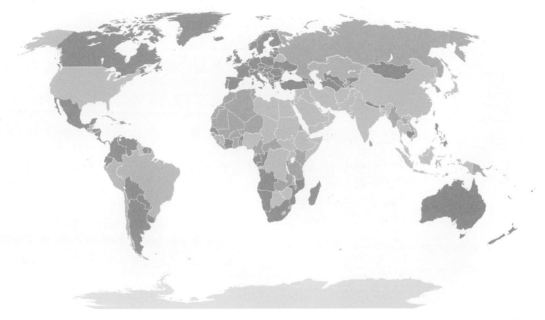

▨ **Retentionist countries** (those countries which have retained the death penalty and executed people): **55**

▨ **Abolitionist countries except for exceptional circumstances** (haven't executed anyone during the last 14 or more years), and abolitionist-in-law for all crimes except those committed under exceptional circumstances (such as crimes committed in wartime): **8**

▨ **Abolitionist-in-practice countries** (haven't executed anyone during the last decade or more and are believed to have a policy or established practice of not carrying out executions): **29**

▨ **Abolitionist countries** (abolitionist in principle, policy and law): **103**

Figure 8.1 World map of the use of the death penalty

However, in 2018, the death penalty was still regularly deployed in 55 countries around the world. A further 37 countries could still legally execute citizens for criminal offences but are thought to have largely abandoned the policy in practice (see Figure 8.1 above). This means that over 60 per cent of the world's population live in countries that retain the death penalty (Ahmed, 2015). The countries that execute the most people are China, Iran, Saudi Arabia and Iraq.

Table 8.1 Countries with the most confirmed executions in 2016

1	China	1000+
2	Iran	567+
3	Saudi Arabia	154+
4	Iraq	88+
5	Pakistan	87
6	Egypt	44+
7	United States	20
8	Somalia	14+
9	Bangladesh	10
10	Malaysia	9

(Amnesty International, 2017)

In 2016, 1032 people were executed in 23 countries. This figure excludes people who were executed in China in 2016 and was lower than the figure recorded by Amnesty International in 2015, when there were 1634 executions in 25 countries (again excluding China) (Amnesty International, 2017). These figures are a considerable underestimate of the real number of executions. It is believed that there are thousands of executions in China every year but there is no reliable data on this. Amnesty International (2011) note that the actual number of deaths sentences in China is a 'state secret': details of executions are not revealed to Chinese citizens and many of those sentenced to death are executed immediately. Although the recorded figure is around 1000 executions a year, many criminal offences in China have a death sentence and it is estimated that China executes six to eight thousand of its citizens every year (Stafford Smith, 2007). In fact, there are significant challenges regarding collation of accurate data on the death penalty in a number of countries. When monitoring bodies such as Amnesty International cite data on 'confirmed executions', a + is often added to the number of deaths. This indicates that the actual number of people executed in that country is higher than the figure officially recorded and disclosed. In 2016, 3117 death sentences were recorded in 25 countries – a significant increase on the 1998 death sentences in 61 countries in 2015 (Amnesty International, 2017). A staggering 18,848 people were 'on death row' (awaiting execution) at the end of 2016.

1.1 The death penalty in the United States

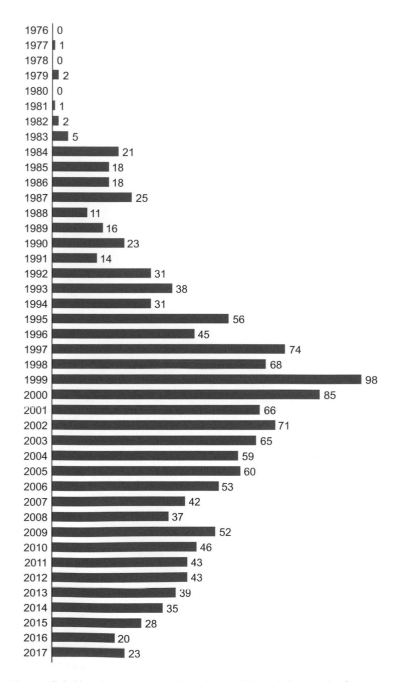

Figure 8.2 Number of executions in the United States in the years 1976–2017

31 of the 50 states of the United States still retained the death penalty in 2018. The United States executed 20 people in 2016 (the lowest

number of executions in the country since 1991) and 23 people in 2017, all by lethal injection. The highest number of executions in the United States was in 1999, when 98 people were executed, of which one third were black (Ford, 2014). The numbers of executions in the last 42 years are detailed in Figure 8.2, which shows that the number of people executed has been on a downward curve since 1999.

In the previous chapter, you considered the ideas expounded by criminologist Stan Cohen in *States of Denial* (2001). Cohen warns of the 'severed head rule' (nobody wants to see pictures of severed human heads) and that too much gruesome information can be a 'switch off', further reinforcing denial. He argues, however, that although we often find ways of blocking out the suffering of others, we should where possible allow 'negative imagery to speak for itself' (p. 185). For Cohen, acknowledgement of human suffering means that sometimes people should be exposed to unpleasant information, or what he refers to as 'unwelcome knowledge'. Human suffering should always be acknowledged, whoever the victim is. This is certainly the case when it comes to acknowledgement of the suffering of victims of intentional homicides and other serious harms, whether they are legally defined as crimes or not.

Chapter 6 highlighted a number of key themes around the denial and acknowledgement of victimhood because of a person's social background or perceived status and 'respectability', and you will explore the victim perspective further in later chapters. Indeed, sometimes unwelcome knowledge about the death penalty is best encountered in autobiographies of people on death row or by those who have visited them, such as *Dead Man Walking* (Prejean, 1993), which was also made into a film in 1995. The fictional Hollywood film *The Green Mile*, a 1999 crime drama based on the 1996 novel by Stephen King, also provides a detailed, factually based account of all the different people involved in state executions: victims and their families, perpetrators and state officials.

Descriptions of the methods used in state executions are also an example of unwelcome knowledge, but they are one important way of shedding a unique light on the actual processes of the death penalty. In the 31 retentionist US states, five forms of execution were still legal in 2018.

The gallows (hanging)

Hanging is the suspension of a person in the air through placing a ligature (traditionally a rope) around their neck. Hanging has a long and controversial history. There were three hangings in the United States between 1976 and 2017 (Death Penalty Information Center, 2018a). In 2018, Washington and New Hampshire were the only two states that still retained the option of hanging.

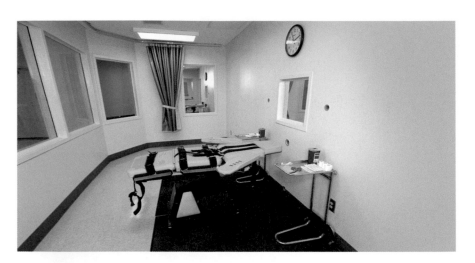

An execution room for lethal injection

Lethal injections were first used in the United States in Texas in 1982 and quickly became the most common method of execution in the United States. There were 1267 lethal injections between 1976 and 2017 (Death Penalty Information Center, 2018a).

The electric chair – sometimes referred to as 'Old Sparky'

The electric chair was introduced in the United States in 1890. There were 158 executions by electrocution between 1976 and 2017 and it was still retained as an option in Alabama, Florida, South Carolina and Virginia in 2018 (Death Penalty Information Center, 2018a).

An execution chamber (firing squad)

The firing squad has only been retained by the state of Utah. The firing squad was used as a method of execution in the United States on three occasions from 1965–2017 (Death Penalty Information Center, 2018a).

The gas chamber

The gas chamber is an airtight room into which poisonous gas is released and has been used to execute prisoners in the United States since the 1920s (Murphy, 2005; Christianson, 2010). The gas chamber was still retained as an option for state execution in three states in 2018: Arizona, Missouri and Wyoming. There were 11 executions by gas chamber between 1976 and 2017 (Death Penalty Information Center, 2018a).

The number of people sentenced to death in the United States decreased to 31 in 2016, which was the lowest number recorded since 1973. There were, however, 2832 people still on death row in the United States in 2018. A disproportionately large number of the people on death row in the United States are black or Latino. The national death-row population is roughly 42 per cent black. This is nearly three times larger than the proportion to the general population, which is around 13.6 per cent black (Ford, 2014).

However, it is important to look not just at the perpetrator, but also the victim, to understand how the death sentence and capital punishments are applied. Roughly half of intentional homicide victims in the United States are black. However, more than three-quarters of the victims of perpetrators executed since 1976 were white (Ford, 2014).

Is the victim white?

- In Louisiana, a defendant is almost twice as likely to receive a death sentence if the victim is white than if the victim is black.

- In California, a defendant is three times more likely to receive a death sentence if the victim is white than if the victim is black, and four times more likely to receive a death sentence if the victim is white than if the victim is Latino.

- In North Carolina, a defendant is three-and-a-half times more likely to receive a death sentence if the victim is white as opposed to those of other ethnicities.

(Death Penalty Information Center, 2018b)

Reflective activity: Racism and the death penalty

In the United States, why do you think that the killing of a white person by a black person is more severely punished? Is the historical context of slavery and racism important in shaping attitudes towards people who perpetrate intentional homicide?

As previously highlighted, not all states in the United States have the death penalty. This has led to interesting observations about the impact that the death penalty has on the rates of crime, especially serious crimes like intentional homicide. There is, however, no evidence that state executions lower the murder rate. The states with the highest murder rates are in the south of the country, but they account for approximately *80 per cent* of all state executions in the United States. The lowest murder rates are in the north-eastern states, which have less than 1 per cent of all state executions (Death Penalty Information Center, 2018b).

Summary

- The majority of the world's population live in countries that retain the death penalty.

- The exact number of executions around the world is not known, but it is estimated to be several thousand every year.

- There are a number of different methods of execution in the United States.

- The death penalty is disproportionately applied in the United States when the victim of intentional homicide is white.

2   Questioning the death penalty: why punish?

The death penalty is a form of state punishment. In particular, when violent interpersonal harms are perpetrated they can cause a deep, emotional response in both observers and victims alike. This, in turn, prompts a call to 'right' that which has been 'wronged' and to make the perpetrator understand – first hand – the nature of the suffering they have caused (de Beauvoir, 1946). In modern day societies, the state is often considered the appropriate agent to deliver punishment to the perpetrator on behalf of the wronged person.

The emotional desire for punishment may be inextricably linked to cultural, moral and philosophical ideals. Thus, it is not clear whether the drive for punishment is an innate human desire or if it is the result of cultural influences. Practices of punishment, however, are long established and well-entrenched in many societies. While it must be recognised that the decision to punish is, in fact, a choice (meaning that any society could choose not to punish), the commonplace use of punishment as a criminal justice response invites consideration of its justification.

Reflective activity: How should we respond to wrongdoing?

Can you think of a time in which you, a friend or family member were wronged in some way? This may be something very small and everyday. Can you remember what you wanted to happen to the person who caused you harm? What, in your opinion, was the best way to make the situation right?

Nicola Lacey, whose work you came across in Chapter 5, has argued that:

> There is no one neat, polished final justification for punishment: there are only arguments for and against it, which apply differently not only within different political systems but also

according to the social and economic conditions holding in different societies in which the institutions exist.

(1988, p. 15)

Despite the fact that there are many different *justifications* for punishment, there are at least three essential ideas present in most modern definitions of punishment:

> Punishment is deliberately administered by state officials on an individual who is legally defined as being subject to the laws of that state. It requires some … justification that the pain/ deprivation/suffering is warranted, because punishment involves intentional deprivation and suffering. The usual view of its primary purpose is that it should be instrumental in reducing or containing rates of criminal behaviour.

(Drake et al., 2010, p. 16)

There are generally five *purposes* of punishment, which fall into two approaches: one is forward-looking and concerned with future harms, the other is backward-looking and argues from a moral position. Each purpose and their definitions are set out below, under their approaches.

Arguments concerned with preventing future harm

Deterrence: the idea of punishment as a deterrence is to deter or discourage people from breaking the law, through the threat of punishment. Aiming to prevent people in society, generally, from committing a crime is referred to as 'general deterrence'. The idea here is that having some consequence in place will prevent the average person from thinking it is a good idea to commit an unlawful act.

Similarly, deterrence is also believed to be achieved by the severity of the punishment experienced by an individual 'offender'. If someone ignores the general deterrence of the threat of punishment and goes on to commit and be convicted of an unlawful act, it is thought that the punishment needs to be severe enough for that individual never to commit an unlawful act again. This is referred to as 'specific deterrence'.

Incapacitation: the idea of incapacitation is, simply, to remove a person from society – to incapacitate them – in order to prevent the person from committing future unlawful acts.

Rehabilitation: rehabilitation is concerned with altering the future behaviour of the 'offender'. It may involve retraining, education, treatment programmes, counselling or other interventions intended to ensure that an individual goes on to lead a law-abiding life.

Moral arguments

Retribution: unlike deterrence, incapacitation, or rehabilitation, the idea of retribution is not concerned with crime prevention or the future unlawful actions of an individual. As discussed in Chapter 5, retribution is a 'backward-looking' reason for punishment: it focuses on making amends for a harm that has already occurred. 'Retributive' punishment is the idea that there needs to be some kind of social retaliation in response to someone having broken the law. It is concerned with rebalancing the social order.

Restitution: the simplest way to think about restitution is that it is a 'pay back' in financial terms. This 'payment' can be made either through time or labour, although often restitution as a punishment is achieved through a fine. Like retribution, it is a form of punishment concerned with 'making amends' for a past misdeed.

These justifications for punishment will be considered in the next section of this chapter, with specific reference to the death penalty.

Summary

- Punishments inflict harm and suffering and, as these contradict basic human values (such as love, forgiveness and compassion), always require justification.

- Forward-looking purposes of punishment are grounded in the prevention of future harms and include deterrence, incapacitation and rehabilitation.

- Backward-looking purposes of punishment are based on moral arguments and include retribution and restitution.

3   Arguments for and against the death penalty

The death penalty is sometimes also referred to as 'capital punishment'. The origin of this phrase comes from the Latin *capitalis*, from *caput* or 'head'. Thus, the phrase 'capital punishment' makes implicit reference to execution by beheading. The death penalty has a very long history and was a key punishment in both ancient Greek and Roman civilisations (Guizot, 1848; Allen, 2002; Bauman, 2004; Hood and Hoyle, 2015). The death penalty has included a number of unusual methods, including crucifixion, drowning, beating, burning alive, burying alive, beheading and impalement.

3.1   Arguments for the death penalty

As with the purposes of punishment, arguments in favour of the death penalty fall into two categories:

- arguments concerned with preventing future harm

- arguments based on morality.

Arguments concerned with preventing future harm

This category is built on arguments concerned with preventing future offences – either by the general population or by a specific individual. There are two main strands to this: *deterrence* and *incapacitation*.

The deterrence argument follows the logic that a threat of death will prevent people from committing any acts that would be met with this punishment. The incapacitation argument is that capital punishment permanently removes a person who has committed murder from society, preventing them from posing a continuing danger to others. This implicitly suggests that there is no hope for change within the person who has offended and, as a result, permanent incapacitation (death) is the only way to ensure that the person never kills another again (Pojman and Reiman, 1997).

These arguments assume that the death penalty strengthens crime-control efforts and that the threat of harm to people will be reduced. In this sense, capital punishment should result in demonstrable evidence of effectiveness, with fewer intentional homicides.

Arguments based on morality

The second category of arguments in favour of capital punishment are those based on morality. Morality can be thought about as a system of values and standards of conduct, often associated with schools of religious thought. It is important to recognise, however, that different moral systems underpin different human cultures: there is not one single code of morality that governs all human societies. Moreover, the effectiveness of different punishments in reducing crime or harm in society is irrelevant from a moral perspective. These arguments are based more on a sense of what people might feel or think is 'right' or 'wrong', which is widely divergent both within and between societies (Pojman and Reiman, 1997).

The next argument in favour of the death penalty to consider, retaliation, is perhaps the most frequently cited: there has to be a rebalancing of the social order, a commensurate or equal form of retaliation (authorised by law). In the Bible, this sentiment was expressed as 'any mischief follows, then thou shalt give life for life, eye for eye, tooth for tooth, hand for hand, foot for foot, burning for burning, wound for wound, stripe for stripe' (Exodus 21: 23–25). There are difficulties in the literal translation of the Bible scripture and, in the original Hebrew, the expression is 'life in place of a life', which could be translated as indicating redress and balance rather than retaliation. However, the literal translation is often repeated as the most persuasive moral justification for the death penalty.

A related argument in favour of the death penalty that also highlights the importance of it as a form of retaliation is that it provides closure for victims. For example, when a person is murdered we may consider their friends and family to also be victims. To assist these victims with overcoming their loss, it is argued that the person who caused their suffering needs to be executed. Again, it is worth pointing out that these 'retributive' arguments in favour of capital punishment are based firmly on a sense of morality as opposed to evidence (Camus, 1957; Pojman and Reiman, 1997). The idea that there should be retaliation when one person wrongs or harms another in order for a society to 'right that which has been wronged' is not the only response. (For example, in Chapter 5, you came across Lacey and Pickard's (2015) argument that forgiveness is an equally human response.) However, the argument for retribution is a very common one.

3.2   Arguments against the death penalty

As before, arguments against the death penalty fall into two categories:

- arguments concerned with preventing future harm

- arguments based on morality.

Arguments concerned with preventing future harm

Timothy Evans, wrongfully executed in 1950

There is very little evidence that the threat of death serves as a deterrent. In countries that have the death penalty for murder, murders still occur. Evidence suggests that capital punishment does not work as a *general* deterrent against the harms it is intended to prevent (Bedau and Cassell, 2005). That is, in jurisdictions that have applied the threat of the death penalty for specific crimes, these crimes still occur at similar rates to places that do not have the death penalty.

Obviously, the death penalty, when applied to a single individual, prevents that person from ever committing a crime again (Bedau, 2001). On this basis, the death penalty 'works' as a *specific* deterrent. It also incapacitates the perpetrator by permanently removing them from society. However, some of the evidence on death penalty cases suggests that there are often miscarriages of justice, wherein someone is executed and later found to be innocent of the crime. It is also impossible to determine if someone would actually commit murder again in the future (Zimring, 2004).

Executing innocent people in the UK

- *George Kelly* was executed in 1950 for the murders of Leonard Thomas and John Catterall during a bungled burglary. His conviction was overturned by the Court of Appeal in June 2003 – judges agreed that the original conviction was 'unsafe'.

- *Timothy Evans* was executed in 1950 for the murder of his daughter. He was, however, officially pardoned in 1966 following a public inquiry chaired by Sir Daniel Brabin (hearings were held between 22 November 1965 and 21 January 1966). The inquiry exonerated him of the murder of his daughter, who had in fact been killed by John Christie.

- *Mahmood Hussein Mattan* was convicted of the murder of Lily Volpert in Cardiff on the basis of one single eyewitness. Mattan, a Somali former merchant seaman, was executed in 1952 but his conviction was quashed in 1998.

- *Derek Bentley* was hanged for murder in 1953 for allegedly killing a police officer during an attempted burglary. He did not fire the shot that led to the death of police officer Frederik Fairfax. He was pardoned in 1993 and his conviction was officially overturned in 1998.

Reflective activity: Justice?

Albert Pierrepoint, a hangman who executed more than 400 people (including miscarriages of justice cases such as Timothy Evans, Derek Bentley and George Kelly), famously wrote that: 'All the men and women whom I have faced at that final moment convince me that in what I have done I have not prevented a single murder' (Pierrepoint, 1974, cited in Berlins, 2006). Do you think that the death penalty is a just or effective way of responding to human wrongdoing?

Arguments based on morality

The death penalty can be argued against on the basis that every human life is valuable. While the loss of a human being at the hands of another is a tragedy, it can be argued that this tragedy will only be compounded if another human life is lost at the hands of the state (Sellin, 1980; Zimring and Hawkins, 1986; Zimring, 2004). Further, it is sometimes argued that the taking of a life through a state execution is an act of hypocrisy that allows the state to legally take a human life in response to a member of society committing the same action. Central for critics is the question of whether the state has the right to deliberately take a person's life (Foucault, 2000; Adelsberg, 2015). Critics also question whether the application of the death penalty is undermined because it is primarily people from poor and impoverished backgrounds who are sentenced to death (Culbert, 2001).

As you saw in the previous chapter, human rights are a means of attempting to limit a state's actions, so it should come as no surprise that the language of rights is deployed *against* the death penalty. The UN, the European Convention on Human Rights (ECHR) and other international human rights bodies point to the importance of the 'right to life'. For them, the death penalty denies the value of human life and leads to direct violations of the right to life. Human rights arguments shine a light on the way in which the state has the power to take life, and questions the right of the state to have such powers.

Summary

- The forward-looking arguments for the death penalty have problems evidencing the claim that the punishment reduces future harms.

- The backward-looking arguments for the death penalty have been criticised as simply an expression of vengeance.

- The arguments against the death penalty emphasise how this punishment violates basic human rights, most importantly the right to life.

- International human rights laws have called for the end of the death penalty around the world since the 1940s.

4   Abolition, state power and criminal law

A number of countries have abolished the death penalty due to increasing international pressure. The European Union has made the abolition of the death penalty a precondition for entry, and Protocol 13 of the ECHR bans the death penalty, even in times of war. In 1997, the UN Commission on Human Rights passed a resolution stating that the 'abolition of the death penalty contributes to the enhancement of human dignity and to the progressive development of human rights'. The call for the end of the death penalty through international human rights covenants is one of the strongest current examples of human rights being used to try and control state power.

From the fifth century to the twentieth century, hanging was the main form of execution in England and Wales (Potter, 1991). Public executions came to an end in 1868, following the recommendations of the Royal Commission on Capital Punishment 1864–66 (Gatrell, 1994). Although there were still large numbers of people executed in prisons from the 1860s onwards, the campaign to end capital punishment gradually gained momentum. The *Children Act 1908* abolished capital punishment for anyone under the age of 16, and in 1933 the minimum age for hanging was raised to 18. This was shortly after the long-standing tradition of not executing pregnant women was enshrined in law in 1931. The *Homicide Act 1957* reduced the scope of executions still further, distinguishing between capital murder (which would lead to execution) and non-capital murder (which would lead to a life sentence in prison).

Following a private member's bill (where a member of parliament introduces a law independently of government) by Labour MP Sidney Silverman in 1965, the *Murder (Abolition of Death Penalty) Act 1965* suspended the death penalty for murder in most of the UK (the exception was Northern Ireland) for five years. On the 16 December 1969, a motion was passed in the House of Commons to make the Act permanent (Block and Hostettler, 1997). The death sentence for murder was finally abolished across the whole of the UK following the *Northern Ireland (Emergency Provisions) Act 1973*.

Although there was some support among the public for a return to the death penalty, when it was debated in the House of Commons in 1983, politicians felt that the arguments in favour of the death penalty were not strong enough to make a plausible case to overturn its virtual abolition (Hird and Kellner, 1983). Hanging officially remained a possible sentence in England and Wales until 1998, at which point the death penalty was abolished for the crimes of piracy and treason in the *Crime and Disorder Act 1998*. The ratification of the ECHR into English law in 1998 with the *Human Rights Act 1998*, means the death penalty is prohibited in the UK while it remains a signatory of the ECHR.

4.1   State-sanctioned murder?

A phrase widely used by anti-death-penalty campaigners sums up the contradiction lying at the heart of the death penalty: 'When you use murder to end murder you guarantee murder will never end'. The death penalty is the intentional killing of an individual by the state. This physical act of taking life is hard to differentiate from intentional homicides. In 1983, the sociologist, Steven Box, published the influential book *Power, Crime and Mystification*, which considered the question of why some very harmful acts and behaviours are illegal and others are not. Like many other criminologists before, he points out that criminal law is defined and established by those who hold the power in a given society. Those with the most privilege and wealth in a society also tend to hold power and, as a result, are more likely to create laws in their own interests.

Importantly, however, Box points out that not all criminal laws favour the interests of the most powerful in society. There are some criminal laws that are in everyone's interests, such as those against murder (intentional homicide), rape, robbery and so on. He argues that everyone benefits from these laws. But, he also argues, there is more to consider when examining criminal law.

> ... the criminal law, definitions of murder, rape, robbery, assault, theft, and other serious crimes are so constructed as to exclude many similar, and in important respects, identical acts, and these are just the acts likely to be committed more frequently by powerful individuals ... We are encouraged to see murder as a particular act involving a very limited range of stereotypical

actors, instruments, situations and motives. Other types of avoidable killing are either defined as less serious crime than murder, or as matters more appropriate for administrative or civil interference.

(Box, 1983, pp. 8–9)

It is estimated that the death penalty leads to thousands of avoidable and premature deaths around the world each year. The perpetrator of this death is the state, which defines the remit of criminal law, which means that nowhere is it defined as a crime: the death penalty is lethal but legal. It is premeditated and follows certain legal procedures. This is a timetabled death. While there is always hope of reprieve prior to the execution, condemned prisoners on death row often experience a 'death of the personality' – where the consciousness of impending death results in the prisoner losing any interest in the future or in past relationships (Johnson, 1981). In a much cited passage, the philosopher Albert Camus states:

> Capital punishment is the most premeditated of murders, to which no criminal's deed, however calculated, can be compared. For there to be an equivalency, the death penalty would have to punish a criminal who had warned his victim of the date on which he would inflict a horrible death on him and who, from that moment onward, had confined him at his mercy for months. Such a monster is not to be encountered in private life.

(1957, p. 199)

Summary

- The act of taking a life is legal via capital punishment, but illegal if it is an intentional homicide.
- The death penalty is sometimes considered by its critics to be even crueller than most intentional homicides.

Conclusion

The majority of the world's population in 2018 still live in countries that retain the death penalty. Some countries, such as the United States, have attempted to execute condemned prisoners as humanely as possible, although, for its critics, the inherent cruelty and inhumanity of any execution can never be removed. In this chapter, the strengths and weaknesses of the ethical justifications for the death penalty have been outlined. The discussion has also highlighted how the death penalty is in opposition to many international human rights norms. For death penalty abolitionists, state executions will always be human rights violations.

The chapter has also located the death penalty within the context of state power and the political justifications of state executions. The state has the power of death over its citizens, and the death penalty is one legal example of this. The defence of the death penalty is dependent upon a distinction between murder (intentional homicide) and execution being successfully made. Focusing on the debates around the death penalty sensitises us to which harms are, and which harms are not, defined as criminal.

References

Adelsberg, G. (2015) 'US racism and Derrida's theologico-political sovereignty', in Adelsberg, G., Guenther, L. and Zerman, S. (eds) (2015) *Death and Other Penalties*, New York, Fordham University Press.

Ahmed, M. (2015) 'Worldwide debate to abolish the death penalty forever', *International Journal of African and Asian Studies*, vol. 14, pp. 139–53.

Allen, D. (2002) *The World of Prometheus: The Politics of Punishing in Democratic Athens*, Princeton, Princeton University Press.

Amnesty International (2011) *Death sentences and executions*, London, Amnesty International [Online]. Available at https://www.amnestyusa.org/reports/death-sentences-and-executions-2011/ (Accessed 14 March 2018).

Amnesty International (2017) 'The death penalty: facts and figures', 11 April [Online]. Available at https://www.amnesty.org/en/latest/news/2017/04/death-penalty-2016-facts-and-figures/ (Accessed 14 March 2018).

Bauman, R. A. (2004) *Crime and Punishment in Ancient Rome*, London, Routledge.

Bedau, H. A. (2001) 'Abolishing the death penalty even for the worst murderers', in Sarat, A. (ed.) (2001) *The Killing State: Capital Punishment in Law, Politics, and Culture*, Oxford, Oxford University Press.

Bedau, H. A. and Cassell, P. (2005) *Debating the Death Penalty: Should America Have Capital Punishment?,* Oxford, Oxford University Press.

Berlins, M. (2006) 'The secret executioner', *Guardian,* 31 March [Online]. Available at https://www.theguardian.com/film/2006/mar/31/1 (Accessed 14 March 2018).

Block, B. and Hostettler, J. (1997) *Hanging in the Balance: A History of the Abolition of Capital Punishment in Britain*, Winchester, Waterside Press.

Box, S. (1983) *Crime, Power and Mystification*, London, Routledge.

Camus, A. (1957) *Resistance, Rebellion & Death (including Reflections on the Guillotine)* (trans. J. O'Brien)*,* New York, Alfred A. Knopf (this edition 1961).

Children Act 1908 (7 Edw. 7, c. 67).

Christianson, S. (2010) *The Last Gasp: The Rise and Fall of the American Gas Chamber*, California, University of California Press.

Cohen, S. (2001) *States of Denial*, Cambridge, Polity Press.

Culbert, J. L. (2001) 'Beyond intention: A critique of the "normal" criminal agency, responsibility and punishment in American death penalty jurisprudence', in Sarat, A. (ed.) (2001) *The Killing State: Capital Punishment in Law, Politics, and Culture*, Oxford, Oxford University Press.

Death Penalty Information Center (2018a) *Methods of execution* [Online]. Available at https://deathpenaltyinfo.org/methods-execution (Accessed 14 March 2018).

Death Penalty Information Center (2018b) *Facts about the Death Penalty*, Washington, Death Penalty Information [Online]. Available at https://deathpenaltyinfo.org/documents/FactSheet.pdf (Accessed 15 March 2018).

de Beauvoir, S. (1946) 'Oeil pour oeil', in Simons, M. A. (ed.) (2004) *Philosophical Writings (Beauvoir Series)*, Chicago, University of Illinois Press.

Drake, D., Muncie, J. and Westmarland, L. (2010) *Criminal Justice: Local and Global*, Cullompton, Willan Publishing/Milton Keynes, The Open University.

Exodus 21: 23–25, New International Version of the Bible.

Ford, M. (2014) 'Racism and the execution chamber', *The Atlantic*, 23 June [Online]. Available at https://www.theatlantic.com/politics/archive/2014/06/race-and-the-death-penalty/373081/ (Accessed 15 March 2018).

Foucault, M. (2000) 'Pompidou's two deaths', in Faubion, J. (ed.) (2000) *The Essential Works of Michel Foucault 1954–1984: Power*, New York, The New Press.

Gatrell, V. A. C. (1994) *The Hanging Tree*, Oxford, Open University Press.

Great Britain. *Murder (Abolition of Death Penalty) Act 1965: Elizabeth II. Chapter 71 (1965)*London, The Stationery Office.

Great Britain. *Crime and Disorder Act 1988: Elizabeth II. Chapter 37 (1988)* London, The Stationery Office.

Great Britain. *Human Rights Act 1998: Elizabeth II. Chapter 42 (1998)* London, The Stationery Office.

Guizot, M. F. (1848 [n.d]) *A General History of Civilisation in Europe. From the Roman Empire till the French Revolution: also A Treatise on the Death Punishments* (trans. unknown), Edinburgh, Chambers [Online]. Available at Hathi Trust Digital Library (Accessed 15 March 2018).

Hird, C. and Kellner, P. (1983) 'The death penalty debate', *New Statesman*, 22 July, p. 6.

Homicide Act 1957 (5 Eliz. 2, c. 11).

Hood, R. and Hoyle, C. (2015) *The Death Penalty: A Worldwide Perspective*, Oxford, Oxford University Press.

Johnson, R. (1981) *Condemned to Die*, Oxford, Elsevier.

Lacey, N. (1988) *State Punishment: Political Principles and Community Values*, London, Routledge.

Lacey, N. and Pickard, H. (2015) 'To blame or to forgive? Reconciling punishment and forgiveness in criminal justice', *Oxford Journal of Legal Studies*, vol. 35, no. 4, pp. 665–96.

Murphy, S. (2005) 'Diagnosis: State-sanctioned murder', *LewRockwell*, 21 March [Online]. Available at https://www.lewrockwell.com/2005/03/stephaniemurphy/state-sanctioned-murder-2/ (Accessed 15 March 2018).

Northern Ireland. *Northern Ireland (Emergency Provisions) Act 1973: Elizabeth II. Chapter 53* (1973) London, The Stationery Office.

Pojman, L. and Reiman, J. (1997) *The Death Penalty: For and Against*, New York, Rowman and Littlefield Publishers.

Potter, H. (1991) *Hanging in Judgment: Religion and the Death Penalty in England* London, Canterbury Press.

Prejean, H. (1993) *Dead Man Walking: An Eyewitness Account of the Death Penalty in the United States*, New York, Vintage Books.

Sellin, T. (1980) *The Penalty of Death*, London, Sage.

Stafford Smith, C. (2007) 'Hanging in the balance', *Guardian,* 1 May [Online]. Available at https://www.theguardian.com/commentisfree/2007/may/01/hanginginthebalance (Accessed 15 March 2018).

United Nations High Commission for Human Rights Resolution, E/CN.4/1997/12 (April 3, 1997).

Zimring, F. (2004) *The Contradictions of American Capital Punishment*, Oxford, Oxford University Press.

Zimring, F. and Hawkins, G. (1986) *Capital Punishment and the American Agenda*, Cambridge, Cambridge University Press.

Acknowledgements

Grateful acknowledgement is made to the following sources. Every effort has been made to contact copyright holders. If any have been inadvertently overlooked the publishers will be pleased to make the necessary arrangements at the first opportunity.

Chapter 1: The Undercroft Image: David Bartlett/Alamy Stock Photo; Graffiti (tagging) Image: South West Images Scotland/Alamy Stock Photo; Graffiti celebrating the violent teenage gang, The Tongs Image: © John Fleming, This file is licensed under the Creative Commons Attribution Licence http://creativecommons.org/licenses/by/3.0/; Beautiful street art or mindless vandalism? Image: imageBROKER/ Alamy Stock Photo; A Belfast mural of Bobby Sands, MP Image: robertharding/Alamy Stock Photo; Older style loyalist mural in Belfast Image: Charles McQuillan/Stringer/Getty Images; A loyalist mural from 2018 Image: © 2018 Gabi Kent

Chapter 2: An anti-Prohibition parade and demonstration in Newark Image: AP/Shutterstock; Protesters at the Scottish parliament Image: Steven Scott Taylor/Alamy Stock Photo; African National Congress election campaign rally in Cape Town Image: Africa Media Online/ Alamy Stock Photo; Public drunkenness Image: © Police Scotland; Grenfell Tower in 2011 before the cladding was added to the building Image: Nick Potts/PA Archive/PA Images; Grenfell Tower after the cladding had been fitted Image: Studio E Architects Ltd.

Chapter 3: Riot police on Upper Parliament Street after riots in Toxteth Image: WENN Rights Ltd/Alamy Stock Photo; Students protest at the tripling of tuition fees Image: Tommy E Trenchard/ Alamy Stock Photo; Workers cleaning up a chemical spill in a West Midlands lake Image: JONATHAN PLANT/Alamy Stock Photo; Bhopal gas disaster Text Box Image: © Luca Frediani, This file is licensed under a Creative Commons Attribution-Share Alike 2.0 Generic Licence, https://creativecommons.org/licenses/by-sa/2.0/ deed.en

Chapter 4: Classic crime/murder mystery books in the window Image: Steven May/Stockimo/Alamy Stock Photo; Understanding how the media reports crime Text Extract: Canadian Resource Centre for Victims of Crime (2018), 'Understanding how the media reports crime', Blog © 1993–2018 Canadian Resource Centre for Victims of Crime;

Crime Scene Cartoon: © Jeff Parker, Courtesy of Cagle Cartoons; A Coca-Cola advertisement in Lebanon Image: Megapress/Alamy Stock Photo; Banksy Text Extract: Courtesy of Pest Control Office, Banksy, Wall and Piece, Brandalism, 2005; The subvertising group 'Brandalism' installed more than 600 subverts Image: Barnbrook & Friends; Brandalism Text Extract: 'Brandalism'. Copyright © 2019 Brandalism Project; Battersby, M. (2012), 'Brandalism: street artists hijack billboards for "subvertising campaign", 17 July, *Independent*. Copyright © *Independent*.; Another sponsor of the 2015 United Nations Climate Change Conference was Air France Image: Brandalism/Revolt Design

Chapter 5: A collage of sensationalist newspaper headlines Image: Allkindza/E+/Getty Images; A Kinder Surprise Image: Julia Ewan/ The Washington Post/Getty Images; Figure 5.1: Adapted from a graph by M Tracy Hunter based upon data from the United Nations Office on Drugs and Crime and The Economist. This file is licenced under the Creative Commons Attribution-Share Alike 3.0 Unported license, https://creativecommons.org/licenses/by-sa/3.0/deed.en; Figure 5.2: © NHS Health Scotland; People hold placards during a silent march Image: Thabo Jaiyesimi/Alamy Stock Photo

Chapter 6: Prisons are places where societies tend to send their poor Image: Fran/Cartoonstock.com; Aggressive looking man with a knife Image: Dunca Daniel Mihai/Alamy Stock Photo; Dr. Harold Shipman Image: Getty Images/Getty Images News/Getty Images/Universal Images Group; The victims' movements of the 1970s Image: © Ellen Shub 2015. All other rights reserved; Three Prison Officers Charged with Assaulting Inmate at Forest Bank Text Extract: Keeling, N. (2017), 'Three prison officers charged with assaulting inmate of Forest Bank', Manchester Evening News [online], 15th September 2017. Copyright © 2019 M.E.N Media; If curiosity killed the cat Image: Richard Sly/CartoonStock.com; Figure 6.1 Image: Adapted from 'Deaths in police custody' (2019), INQUEST Charitable Trust, Casework and Monitoring Data, www.inquest.org.uk; Christopher Alder (1960–1998) Image: Image used by kind permission of Janet Alder; Janet Alder Image: Fiona Hanson/PA Archive/PA Images

Chapter 7: Thousands of shoes collected by the Nazis from the victims of genocide at Auschwitz Image: Edward North/Alamy Stock Photo; Devastation in Aleppo as a result of the Syrian civil war Image: ZUMA Press, Inc./Alamy Stock Photo; A 'deviant' tattooed man Image (Left): ifulfoto.com/Alamy Stock Photo; Traditional tattoos on face of a Maori warrior (Right): Tim Graham/Alamy Stock Photo;

Demonstrators in Tunisia Image: Str/EPA/REX/Shutterstock; Mural from Article 1, Universal Declaration of Human Rights Image: PvE/Alamy Stock Photo

Chapter 8: Figure 8.1: Adapted from Kamalthebest, This file is licensed under the Creative Commons Attribution-Share Alike 4.0 International licence, https://creativecommons.org/licenses/by-sa/4.0/deed.en; Figure 8.2: Adapted from 'Facts about the Death Penalty', 12th March 2019, Death Penalty Information Center. Copyright © 2019 Death Penalty Information Center; The gallows (hanging) Image: *** From the series The Omega Suites, © Lucinda Devlin 2018; An execution room for lethal injection Image: California Department of Corrections and Rehabilitation; The electric chair Image: Jim West/jimwestphoto.com; An execution chamber (firing squad) Image: Reuters/Trent Nelson-Salt Lake Tribune/Pool; The gas chamber Image: Science Photo Library; Timothy Evans, wrongfully executed in 1950 Image: George Elam/Daily Mail/REX/Shutterstock

Index

50   Intro

150   Def   ←————   Citation

250   Ex 1   2 ————   citation

250   Ex 2   2 ————   citation

50   Conclusion

Ref list

———————————————————

• Video and audio!
   Stop, take notes. Go Back reflect on notes
   adequate? Gaps? Misunderstandings?

• Same method re Textbook.

• Also → write in margins key points
   of a paragraph.

OR   Highlighter pen → do same!